John Bevis

The Keartons
Inventing nature photography

Uniformbooks 2016

Frontispiece: *"Wren going into her nest in rick"*.

First published 2016
Copyright © John Bevis
ISBN 978–1–910010–09–9

Uniformbooks
7 Hillhead Terrace, Axminster, Devon EX13 5JL
www.uniformbooks.co.uk

Trade distribution in the UK by Central Books
www.centralbooks.com

Printed and bound by T J International, Padstow, Cornwall

Contents

Introduction   7

1. At home with the Keartons   19
2. The first nature photography book   37
3. The Kearton partnership   57
4. The stuffed ox and other hides   85
5. The man who shot Roosevelt in Africa   107
6. Deceiving wild creatures   129
7. The wildness of wild life   147

Notes   169
Bibliography and filmography   173
References   181
Acknowledgements   185
Index   187

The Keartons

I first came across the names of
the Kearton brothers, Richard and
Cherry, on the cover of a green cloth-
bound book picked out of a box at
a jumble sale in Kenley, Surrey. The
title, *Wild Nature's Ways*, suggested
one of those familiar, worthy
collections from the early 1900s of
sentimental musings on the English
countryside and wildlife. Leafing
through the pages I found, sure
enough, charming portraits of birds
and other small creatures, flitting
their way through chapters devoted
to 'woodland and hedgerow' or
'broadland and streamside'. Near the
front of the book, the pages fell open

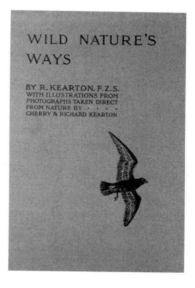

at a full-page plate of a cow standing in a field. Wondering how this
rather wooden-looking farm animal earned its place in a book about
wild nature, I took a second look. There was a caption: "The Stuffed
Ox in Operation". I had no idea what it meant, except that it was
neither familiar nor sentimental. I bought the book immediately.

That was the start of a long and enjoyable curiosity about the
Keartons and their work as pioneering nature photographers, satisfied in small and occasional doses by collecting one after another of
their books on cycling trips around London's second-hand bookshops.
Both of the Keartons, funnily enough, had lived and worked within a
couple of miles of the Kenley village hall where my quest had begun.
As for the stuffed ox, it was, I learned, one of a family of photographic
hides they had constructed for the purpose of allowing the photographer and camera to encroach unseen on the territory of the nesting
or feeding bird. It is, perhaps, their best-known creation, the panto-
mime creature that hobbles on stage whenever the name of Kearton
is called from the wings.

The brothers, showmen that they were, documented the use of the hide in a series of photographs, taken in the spring of 1900, showing the ox's strength (with Cherry mounted on its back), portability (hoisted over his shoulder), and vulnerability (inverted on the ground having been blown over by the wind, with Cherry inside, all six legs kicking up in the air). To modern eyes these images, in which the Keartons' deadpan humour is reinforced by solemn expressions and their antiquated dress code of tweed suits and ties, suggest stills from early silent comedy films; the absurd hides themselves seem to anticipate the harebrained logic of W. Heath Robinson. Not surprising, then, to find a common perception of the Keartons as the merry pranksters of nature photography, eccentrics with the gift of making us laugh with their ever more weird and wonderful apparatus.

But behind the occasional wackiness was a serious intent. In 1947, Eric Hosking proclaimed the Keartons "the fathers of natural history photography".[1] Peter Scott was presented with his first book at school by Cherry Kearton, and recorded later that he was "naturally grateful to the pioneer who led me to so much enjoyment".[2] At the age of eight, David Attenborough was taken to see *Dassen*, a film lecture presented by Cherry Kearton which "captured my childish imagination and made me dream of travelling to far-off places to film wild animals".[3] Eric Ashby, Stuart Smith and Ralph Chislett are among many other eminent nature photographers of their generation to have corresponded with and been inspired by the Kearton brothers.

What made them so influential is, in part, the simple tally of the 'firsts' they notched up. Cherry Kearton's first stab at nature photography, at Boreham Wood in 1892, produced the first ever photo of a nest with eggs. On the back of that shot, they published *British Birds' Nests: How, Where and When to Find and Identify Them*, the first nature book illustrated entirely with photographs, and forerunner of a series of best-selling books written by Richard and illustrated with photographs taken 'direct from nature', as the jackets and title pages crowed, by Cherry. Richard Kearton, of course, invented the concept of the portable photographic hide, in a series of experiments of which the stuffed ox was the most magnificent. Cherry, the younger of the two brothers, made the first field sound recording of a wild bird singing, in 1900, and went on to take the first film footage of London from the air in 1908, of species of big game in Africa in 1909, and of hostilities at the outbreak of World War I in Belgium.

Right: *"Female sparrow hawk and young"*.

Richard laid claim to making a number of nature discoveries, and to resolving through photographic evidence several disputations. He proved, for example, that the sparrowhawk can build its own nest, rather than invariably taking over the old nest of a crow or wood pigeon; that the under mandible of the wryneck is longer than the upper one; that "the female red-necked phalarope wears a white dot, and the male a white streak, over either eye"; that a male adult bird will sometimes feed the chicks of an entirely different species.[4] Kearton films showed for the first time how a grass snake will sham death when it considers itself in danger; how a grouse may remove her eggs from the nest and then return them; and how an adder bites.

None of these achievements alone was perhaps enough to earn the Keartons Eric Hosking's accolade. What did was the way they popularised their subject by themselves becoming popular. They helped create, and then corner, the market for nature books by writing for children, young people and adults, in story books, field guides, picture books and essays in adventure and observation. They spurred others to emulate what they did themselves, and were generous in offering advice and sharing the trade secrets of their techniques and equipment. Between them, the brothers produced more nature photography books than any of their contemporaries. Richard became the most sought-after and engaged lecturer of his day on the public circuit; the brothers kindled an enthusiasm for nature in thousands of audiences across the British Isles and beyond, over the course of forty years.

Their other legacy is, of course, the quality of their work. They were prolific and fastidious photographers who as early as 1907 had notched up more than 10,000 plates, including numerous good and some outstanding studies. Eric Hosking and Harold Lowes gave them pride of place in their influential survey *Masterpieces of Bird Photography*. In many of their books we find plates that suggest an originality and ingenuity beyond their journeyman brief. They did not always break new ground; their first photographic mission, to record the nests and eggs of all breeding bird species in Britain, was still under way when other photographers such as R. B. Lodge were already turning their attention to the birds themselves. But they were the first professionals, and that they achieved so much, and are still remembered and valued, is due to the systematic approach they took to their task, funded by their stores of energy, tenacity, originality, insight and enthusiasm.

Left: *"Leverets in their form… the tuft of grass was opened out so as to show the animals"*.

There is an extra dimension to the Keartons which is a little less easy to define. It has to do with a charisma that pervades, if not all of their work, then at least the better part of the output of their partnership. Opening one of their books from this time is exciting because we don't know what we are going to find inside: sometimes it is a photograph that is so beautifully composed, with such elegance of proportion, to reach above and beyond expectation. Sometimes it is a study from nature interpreted through the camera in such a way as to take on a life, and meaning, of its own. Or it may be something so slight that we are amazed that it was noticed at all, let alone made subject of a photograph. These surprises and fascinations have endeared the Keartons to a modern audience; however much they may have been of their time, their sensibilities align comfortably with modern practices such as conceptual art, especially the evidence (often photographic)-based work of landscape artists such as Richard Long and Hamish Fulton, or the sifting and cataloguing of natural phenomena seen in the work of, for example, Chris Drury or the Dutch artist Herman de Vries. The enthusiastic reaction of many writers and artists on mention of their names suggests they have earned a place in the pantheon of those landmark originals worth knowing and talking about.

So it is no surprise to find instances of their material co-opted elsewhere: Kearton sections may be found in, for example, the books accompanying two Scottish Arts Council touring exhibitions, 'The Unpainted Landscape' in 1987, and 'Camouflage' the following year, while a poetry collection by Jeremy Over, published by Carcanet in 2009, features a cover image of Cherry Kearton shouldering the stuffed ox, and borrows a Kearton title: *Deceiving Wild Creatures*. This points up the relative ease with which parallels may be drawn between Kearton and other practices: an instance is the way their photographic documentation of their own photographic exploits—such as the famous example of Cherry aloft on Richard's shoulders deploying the camera on an extended tripod (see p.56)—finds a niche in the history of "the ways in which photography has been used, not just to record, but to transform artistic performances". There is a hint that an image of Cherry Kearton with camera and tripod, abseiling the overhang of a cliff and swinging from the rope in mid-air, nurtures the Kearton myth in much the way that Yves Klein's notorious 1960 image 'Leap Into the Void', in which the artist appeared to hurl himself from the gatepost of a suburban house, was an act "conceived by the artist specifically for its photographic qualities".[5]

Right: *"A perilous descent".*

The core scientific community has at times been more sceptical of the Keartons' populism. By way of illustration, some years ago I asked the librarian at the Natural History Museum, London, if they would be interested in adding to their then incomplete Kearton book section. She told me that in the recent past questions about objectivity, exemplified by the various Kearton story, pet and menagerie books, were seen as compromising, and the library would only have admitted the field guide and observation titles. But latterly, the histories of human interaction with nature, and of the groundswell of popular interest in the natural sciences, were themselves becoming recognised as being of import—not least for the impact that attendant donations and subscriptions have made to funding conservation and research—and a more holistic approach to the work of cheerleaders such as the Keartons was now considered both appropriate and valuable.

Critical attention to the Keartons to date has tended to take the form of academic studies that use them and specific aspects of their work as exemplars to substantiate critical theses. There have also been periodical local history studies, detailed in 'References' below, particularly those relating the Keartons' connections to Yorkshire, published by the *Dalesman*, and to Surrey, by the Bourne Society. Otherwise, most of what has been written about the Keartons concentrates especially on the numerous adventures, dangers, narrow escapes and comic moments they ran into in the course of pursuing their vocation, illustrated by the picturesque quirkiness of their hides and quaint photographic equipment. All of this is well documented in the original books, produced in sufficient quantities that none are particularly rare and, with a little rummaging on the internet, almost all can be obtained today at prices little more than the cost of a new paperback; e-books of many titles may be downloaded cheaply or for free. In addition, and very usefully, Dr W. R. Mitchell has produced a life-and-work study of the Keartons, *Watch the Birdie!*, that sifts the key facts from their books, with additional material from interviews with some of those who knew and corresponded with them. For these reasons, there seems little point in retelling anecdotes worn smooth with age.

I'm writing this at about the time of the seventy-fifth anniversary of the death of Cherry Kearton and, at this distance, it feels the time is right for a reappraisal, to give some critical voice to their legacy as photographers, writers, film makers, and professional partners.

Left: *"Nesting site of nuthatch… a lime and chestnut avenue, Torquay, Devon"*.

As its title is intended to suggest, this book concerns itself with the lives and working partnership of 'The Keartons', especially their role in the history of nature photography; attitudes to and interaction with nature; and the status of invention in their work. I've taken as the core to this book the period of their active collaboration, the years 1892–1908, whose characteristics and achievements formulate our idea of 'The Kearton partnership'. A handful of the photographs taken in this period, I would argue, go some way beyond the usual concerns of the nature photographer; the significance of these was the subject of a previous essay, *Direct from Nature* (1992 & 2007), whose text I have borrowed from here. The partnership is bracketed by two significant moments in their professional lives, each deserving a dedicated chapter. The first covers the events leading up to, and aftermath of, the publication in 1895 of 'The first nature photography book', *British Birds' Nests: How, Where and When to Find and Identify Them*. The second, marking the end of the partnership and Cherry's reinvention as international wildlife film-maker, is 'The man who shot Roosevelt in Africa'. An intermediary chapter, 'The stuffed ox and other hides', examines some of the most remarkable products of their collaboration.

Praise for the Keartons was not always unqualified. David Attenborough recorded being inspired by Kearton's film despite "all its obvious flaws",[6] while at the age of twelve, Eric Ashby detected that in a Cherry Kearton film about Africa "not all the animals were behaving naturally, which to his mind was what nature films should really represent".[7] More recent commentators have, quite literally, taken apart some of Cherry's footage, frame by frame. Veracity and authenticity are the backbone of nature photography, and the questions raised about these aspects of the Kearton opus are examined in a separate chapter, 'Deceiving wild creatures'.

Central to the work of the Keartons, as with all serious nature photography, is the attitude taken to wildlife, in particular animal welfare, conservation and collecting, and how these are affected by the role of photography, in particular within the territory that nature shares with culture, and including cultural interpretations such as anthropomorphism. These are examined in a final chapter, 'The wildness of wild life'.

Most of the published biographical information about the home life of the Keartons and their families is derived from what they wrote themselves, which concentrates on previous generations of their "picturesque forebears" in the Yorkshire Dales, and is sufficiently incomplete for some misapprehensions to have crept in. A little research has uncovered a deal of fresh unpublished material about the brothers and their siblings, married life and immediate descendants. While this may not have much bearing on their careers, it can help us to picture them, and it would seem an opportunity missed to omit this information from the current volume; to it is added a biographical outline of each of the two brothers' lives, including their activities and achievements away from the focus of this book. These are gathered in a stand-alone chapter, 'At home with the Keartons'.

The main purpose of the book is to weigh up how the Keartons achieved such a reputation among their peers, and how well their work has stood the test of time; to ask whether they are best remembered as fathers of their discipline or, as one bookseller I spoke to put it, "those crazy guys who used to take photos from inside a hollow cow".

CHAPTER ONE

At home with the Keartons

The North Yorkshire valley of Swaledale, in the area around Thwaite and Muker, derives its distinctive field-plan through the local tradition of a farm being divided among the sons, the divisions becoming ever smaller down the generations. Hence the meadows and lower slopes of the valley compartmentalised by high limestone walls into tidy rectangles, each with its stone barn, almost like miniature parishes and chapels. Above, the austere monotones of moorland, wilderness in sway with grazing and grouse; along the floor of the valley, thin strands of habitation entwining the ribbon of the Swale. A scrupulous panorama, made picturesque as much from nature's bounty as from the meticulous apportionment of sons' and brothers' properties.

The Keartons of Swaledale were a staunch Wesleyan working clan, who could trace their lineage through generations of gamekeepers, farmers and miners, and their migrations within a few miles and a handful of hamlets and villages up and down the reaches of the Swale. But in 1855, John (Jack) Kearton, a 23-year-old yeoman farmer and gamekeeper, married out, to Mary Hunter of Winton. Mary was not from North Yorkshire but the eastern fringes of Westmoreland (hereafter Cumbria), her family scattered around the pockets of Ravenstonedale, Mallerstang, Nateby, Kirkby Stephen, and on up past Winton to Brough. The area knows itself by its uplands—the Fells— while the Dales are named for their valleys; unlike the neat parallels of the Dales, the landscape here is bitty and arbitrary, the wild and the domestic more mixed up, the River Eden flowing in the 'wrong' direction: north.

Jack and Mary's children, born with the itchy temperament of the borderlands, numbered six: Jane, born 1856; Foster, 1858; Margaret, 1860; Richard, 1862; John, 1866; and the youngest in the family, Cherry, born in 1871. They were raised in a modest stone semi-detached cottage, now named Corner House, in Thwaite, and educated at the National School a mile's walk away in the village of Muker.

Left: *"Snaring grouse"*.

Swaledale is generally marked as their spiritual home, their true north; but in adult life, the three eldest spent more of their time in Cumbria; Richard, who declared "I love my mother's country in the heart of Fell-land with a passion that can never die",[1] was equally at home both sides of the border; while when the two youngest went 'home' later in life, to visit or to live, it was to the Dales.

Richard has described how, "before he was ten years of age", climbing to see inside a bird's nest he fell, dislocating his hip. He was taken to the back room of a pub in Kirkby Stephen, where a drunken bonesetter made a terrible botch of aligning the joint. One consequence was that Kearton was left permanently disabled with one leg several inches shorter than the other; another, less disadvantageous, was that much of the time he was obliged to take off school was spent in the company of his paternal grandfather. Cherry Kearton, born 1792, a Wesleyan lay preacher and bird lover, was incidentally the first of numerous male Keartons to be so christened, in honour of his own mother, Agnes Cherry. He grounded a precocious country lore and bird knowledge in the young Richard, who became adept at tickling trout and "knew where to find the nest of every species breeding in our neighbourhood and to distinguish the cry of any feathered friend almost as soon as it was uttered".[2]

Richard left school aged sixteen, to go into sheep farming on the family's "acre or two of our own, and two small farms rented from different landlords".[3] In 1882, acting as guide to a grouse-shooting party up from London, he took the guns up near the Buttertubs Pass. It was a dull grey day with precious little game to be seen. Sydney Galpin, a publisher, asked if anything could be done about it, whereupon Richard called up an old moorcock by imitating the hen's cry. Galpin was so impressed that on the spot he offered Richard a post in London, to which Kearton's Dickensian answer was, as he reported many years later, "Yes, certainly, sir, if you think you can obtain for me a post to which my intelligence and scanty education will be equal".[4]

On 10 October 1882, Richard Kearton started at Cassell, Petter & Galpin's Ludgate Hill offices at La Belle Sauvage (named for the historic coaching inn that had occupied the same spot and where, curiously, a stuffed rhinoceros, the first specimen to be shown in England, had been exhibited in 1684). He began at the bottom, addressing envelopes, and living in the "heartbreaking discomfort" of digs in Clerkenwell for a few months before taking a room with a "decent family" in Camberwell.[5]

Having completed a shorthand class at Birkbeck Institute, he was promoted to correspondence clerk at Cassell, and found himself

Above: *Richard Kearton's sons, with butterfly nets, c.1911.*

surrounded by some of the eminent writers of the day, including Rider Haggard, W. E. Henley, Grant Richards, Robert Louis Stevenson and William Morris. Oscar Wilde edited *The Woman's World* from the same offices, and Kearton was charmed by the "scintillating brilliance" that "sometimes flashed from a rather dull, heavy face like forked lightning from a thunder-cloud".[6] To continue his education, meanwhile, Kearton read a leading article every day, made a list of unfamiliar words and "by the aid of a dictionary, familiarized myself with their use and meaning".[7]

Crisis struck in 1887, when Jack Kearton died at the age of 55, leaving Mary without support. Jane, then aged 31, and Margaret, 27, were unmarried and living at home; John, 21, was on a labourer's wage, while Cherry, aged 15, was about to leave school. According to the mores of conventional family hierarchy, it was the responsibility of the eldest son to take charge. But Foster, who worked as a game-keeper, was by this time married and raising a family of his own in Muker with his wife Jane (née Brunskill). Foster's eldest daughter Mary would die in 1891, aged six, as would both Jane and the second daughter, Margaret Jane, in October of the following year. The turn of the century saw Foster working as a coal miner and lodging with his two remaining children at Brough, Cumbria, in the household of a charwoman, Emma Atkinson. One of her three young children

Above: *Richard Kearton and his sons, c.1906.*

was christened Lawrence Kearton Atkinson. By 1911, the ménage had moved to the coal-mining village of Edmondsley, County Durham, Foster working as an "underground store man" and now head of household with Emma as housekeeper; Foster's children from his marriage had left home, and there was a further addition to the Atkinson clan, Irene. Foster died at Craghead in 1920.

So it fell to Richard, at the age of 25, to assume the role of father to the family. He secured a post for young Cherry as commercial clerk at Cassell where he started in the autumn of 1887, and moved most of the family down to London, where he had found suitable if modest lodgings at 14 Rose Villas, Hornsey Park Road, just round the corner from where he was himself then living in Malvern Road. In 1891, Mary was matriarch of the Rose Villas household, whose other residents were Jane, Margaret, John and Cherry. There was also a daughter to Jane, Ann, who had arrived in 1888, and the move to London might have been thought to protect Jane's status as a single mother from the attentions of a close-knit rural community. Mary, the two daughters and Ann subsequently returned north, not to Thwaite but to Cumbria, where they shared a little four-roomed cottage in Nateby. Mary died in January 1895 and was buried at St Mary's, Muker, in a blizzard; the funeral procession covered "sixteen miles across the highest and wildest part of the Pennine Range"[8] with the coffin lashed to a sledge, a symbolic haul from Cumbria back to the Dales. Ann, when she came of age, would go into service with a local farming family in Mallerstang; the sisters lived on at the cottage, working as char-women, Jane dying aged 82 in 1939, while Margaret lived to the age of 91. John, described by his brother Richard as "the most powerful man physically I have ever known",[9] took a job as meat porter at Smithfield, and married his neighbour Frances Adelaide Bullock, a dressmaker, on Christmas Day, 1895; brother Cherry was best man. The couple were given a floor of the Bullock family home at 35 Hornsey Park Road,

Above: *Grace Kearton, c.1904.*

where a son, another Cherry, was born in 1896. By 1911, mother and son were living there alone; John, still married to Frances, had returned to Swaledale to work as farm labourer in Gunnerside, where he "ruined his heart and died suddenly while comparatively young" in 1915. The son, Cherry, died of wounds sustained while serving with the Royal West Surreys in the trenches at Arras in April 1917. Frances subsequently became a member of Richard's household, serving as companion to his daughter Dora. She died in 1949.

In 1889, Richard married Ellen Rose Cowdrey, an artist from Hornsey, then aged 29, at St John the Evangelist, Hammersmith. They set up home at 70 Westbeech Road, Edmonton, before moving to Boreham Wood. The couple went on to have five children, of whom the eldest, Dora (1890–1960) was born by a breeches birth which left her permanently disabled; at the age of 15 she had an operation to straighten her legs, but depended for the rest of her life on the care provided firstly by her parents, then Frances, and eventually her sister, Grace. Two years Dora's junior, Grace went on to become Richard's secretary and an accomplished nature photographer in her own right, contributing to three of Richard's books and showing work at the Royal Photographic Society annual exhibitions in 1913 and 1914. In 1921, she married the Surrey naturalist Howard (C. H.) Bentham; they lived at Tadworth, and had a daughter, Margaret. Grace died at Epsom in 1978. Of Richard and Ellen's three sons, Richard (Dick),

1898–1970, was commissioned as 2nd Lieutenant in the Royal Flying Corps, serving in France as an observer flying reconnaissance sorties in RE8s with 52 and 15 Squadrons. Returning to live in Caterham, he worked in banking, and married Minnie Elizabeth Cobb; they had two children. Like Dick, John (Jack) born 1900, trained as an observer (although probably too late to see active service) and went into banking. He lived for a while in the 1920s in Liberia, and became an amateur natural history photographer and lecturer, author of *Bird Life in England* (1931) and *Nature Memories* (1950), and co-author with Hugh Walwyn of *Nature Smiling Through* (1934). John lived at home until his mother's death, before moving to Purley, where he died in 1960. The youngest son, Cherry (who was known to his father as Plod, but referred to himself as Cherry Kearton II), was born in 1901 and went into publishing, becoming director of Hutchinson and managing director of Jarrolds; he was married to Doris Baines, and they had three children. He died at Caterham in 1989.

By the time of his marriage, Richard had been promoted to the position of sub-manager of the publicity department at Cassell, a post he was to occupy until 1898 when he was obliged to retire from ill-health brought on by a bout of influenza the previous winter. Richard and Ellen moved in that year to the therapeutic air and convenient railway connections of Caterham Valley, where it cuts through the Surrey North Downs, first to an apartment of Ardingley Villas, and then in a final move in the spring of 1906 to the ten-room Ashdene, 169 Croydon Road. Formerly the premises of G. Kane, a monumental mason, Ashdene has been described by Richard's grandson as "a lovely house", and by his granddaughter as "a happy, family home", with "photographic dark rooms in the cellar" and "a large garden, an orchard, and free-range chickens running around".[10]

Richard published his first book, *Birds' Nests, Eggs, and Egg Collecting*, in 1890, and his reputation is built on his success as principal author of twenty-one nature-related titles. The second of these, *British Birds' Nests*, with plates by his brother Cherry, was the first true nature photography book. The Keartons' subsequent titles, which included books of observation and anecdote, identification guides, picture books, and stories and non-fiction for children, were all illustrated by photographs shot by members of the Kearton family: Cherry, Richard, and later Richard's children Grace and John. Richard was the inventor of the mimetic bird hide and principal agent of its evolution into the conventional tent hide. With Cherry, he was an early pioneer of nature film photography, and began using colour photography from 1909. He gave his first public lecture "with

Limelight Illustrations" at East Finchley Congregational Literary Society on 15 March 1897, to promote a new title, *With Nature and a Camera*. Such was its success that platform lecturing with magic lantern slides or film projection would soon provide his principal income as, with his "fine voice and a fund of good humour",[11] he went on to become, in his own words, "cock of the walk", for several years the most sought-after circuit lecturer of his day for "universities, schools, learned societies and popular audiences". Richard made a number of trips abroad: to America in April 1908, where he lectured at the White House on invitation from President

Above: *"Our camera", 1898.*

Theodore Roosevelt; a birdwatching trip to Norway in June 1911 with Howard Bentham, and another, to Texel Island, Netherlands, with his daughter Grace, in June 1914. He also lectured on the continent, including visits to Berlin and Paris. In 1917, he was empanelled by the Board of Inventions & Research (forerunner of the Royal Naval Scientific Service) to advise on a scheme for training gulls to associate periscopes with food, so that by flocking they would give away the presence of enemy submarines when they broke surface. Richard was of the opinion that the plan was unmanageable, and it was abandoned. Otherwise, most of the last thirty years of his life followed a routine well described by his son Cherry:

> "From September to the end of March, he was lecturing sometimes four or five days a week with long journeys in between. In the spring and early summer he was away on field work collecting material for his new book and a new lecture. He would start his book sometime in July and finish it by the middle of August and then start preparing his slides and films for the lecture season—a frantically busy life which was largely the cause of his comparatively early death at the age of sixty six".[12]

Above: *"Richard Kearton with jackdaws"*, *c.1925*.

The priorities of Richard's later years are suggested in the proportions of his autobiography, *A Naturalist's Pilgrimage*. After detailing in the first two sections his "picturesque forebears", early life, employment at Cassell, writing and photography, he devoted the third—comprising almost one half of the total volume—to anecdotes surrounding his experiences as a lecturer.

Richard Kearton died of a heart attack at home on 8 February 1928. Ellen died on 16 November 1944.

Having taken his first nature photograph at Enfield in 1892, Richard's brother Cherry supplied all the plates for Richard's earliest photographic nature books, six books in six years. He continued working at Cassell until 1897 or '98 when, faced with an ultimatum to choose between his post and the photography which was keeping him increasingly away from the office, he took the plunge to become a professional photographer. Unable to earn a living purely from nature work, he supplemented the income from Richard's books with portrait, pet and advertising photography. He began taking moving pictures around 1903; was delivering public lectures by 1908; and from 1913 became a published author, writing seventeen book titles in his lifetime.

Cherry was married at Godstone on 7 June 1900, to Mary Burwood Coates. The Coates family were from Gunnerside, a few miles down Swaledale from the Kearton home in Thwaite. Mary's father, William Coates, had a factory in Wood Street, Aldermanbury, which made travel blankets, mantels, and other luxury products of wool shipped from the Dales. It was a lucrative business, on whose proceeds Coates acquired a 10-bedroom mansion, Garston House, on the Godstone Road in Kenley, where Cherry and Mary lived in the months after their marriage. They moved next to Southcote, Merstham; lived from 1903 to 1911 in Foxley Road, Kenley, at a house named for the mountain above Thwaite, Shunnerfell; and had a house on Selhurst Road, South Norwood, around 1912–13. There were two children: a son, Edward Cherry, was born in July 1908; he went on to marry Patience Geraldine I. Wood in 1935, and they had a daughter, Morella. Edward Cherry died at Kington, Herefordshire, in 1974. Cherry and Mary's daughter, Mary Nina (known as Nina), born on Christmas Eve, 1909, married Montague Simpson in 1935 and they had two children; Nina would live to the age of ninety-four, dying at Kingston Hill.

Cherry's work as a photographer in the early years of his marriage involved much travelling within the British Isles, including numerous assignments for Richard, contributing to a further seven books within the years 1902–10. In his own right, in 1900 he acquired a an Edison Bell wax-cylinder sound recorder and repeater to capture animal sounds, and succeeded in making the first ever sound recording of birds singing in the wild, a nightingale and a song thrush at Kenley. He began using a film camera independently of his work with Richard, taking his first cine footage at Boreham Wood in 1903, and securing a moving picture of a whitethroat in 1905. In May 1908, Kearton took the first aerial cine photos of London from the Spencer brothers' airship as a commission for Charles Urban Trading Company.

Cherry took a trip to Algeria 'for health reasons' in the early 1900s, and to Scandinavia with Mary's brother Calvert in 1902 or 1903. In 1909 he was away from home for seven or eight months on his first

Above: *Cherry Kearton filming a crocodile on the shores of Lake Victoria, c.1929.*

African safari, in the company of another of Mary's brothers, William James Coates, FZS, later recruiting the services of naturalist and taxidermist James L. Clark of the New York Natural History Museum. Shots of wildlife great and small, and scenes of natives at work and play, were put together with footage of Theodore Roosevelt being entertained at a native war dance, and of his safari party breaking camp, as the only film record of the ex-President's great safari, Kearton's first feature-length film, *Roosevelt in Africa*. Thereafter his professional life was that of big game photographer and film-maker. The following year Kearton "secured the first moving pictures ever taken of lions in their native haunts"[13] when he was commissioned to film the bizarre Buffalo Jones big-game lassoing safari in British East Africa in 1910. He stayed on to pursue some of the big game that had evaded his camera in 1909, becoming "the only white man who has ever accompanied the Masai in a fight [a lion hunt with spears], without carrying a weapon".[14] The following year saw Kearton in Singapore, India, and North British Borneo where he "was lucky enough to get the first picture of the orang-outang at home in the jungle".[15] In 1912 he filmed moose in Canada, travelling via Long Island and Yellowstone Park, where he obtained footage of bison and black bears. Kearton returned to Africa in April 1913, to undertake a twelve-month expedition with James Barnes "across Africa from East to West", starting at Mombasa and retracing in part the route taken by H. M. Stanley, travelling "some twelve hundred miles down the River Congo" to reach journey's end at the Congo sea port of Matadi. He was in Belgium in August 1914, and spent much of the first two months of the war securing the first film records of military action and its effects on civilian life. He witnessed at first hand the siege of Antwerp, escaping at the last minute by steamboat down the Scheldt estuary to the Dutch frontier, and then on to the North Sea port of Vlissingen by "transfer to the railway—indeed I travelled to Flushing on the footboard, hanging on precariously with one hand on the frame of a window".[16]

In February 1915, aged 44 and lately much increased in girth, Cherry Kearton was commissioned as First Lieutenant, 25th Battalion Royal Fusiliers (Legion of Frontiersmen) under Colonel Driscoll, and would serve for three years in German East Africa. The Legion of Frontiersmen was a patriotic paramilitary organisation formed in 1905, in response to fears of an invasion of Britain, as a field intelligence corps of Empire loyalists. Eminent early Frontiersmen included explorers Ernest Shackleton, Captain Scott and 'Titus' Oates; authors Edgar Wallace, Erskine Childers, Sir Arthur Conan Doyle, H. Rider Haggard and Rudyard Kipling; and leading public figures such as Lord Kitchener and Jan Smuts. A founding member was Robert Baden-Powell, and the principles—and headgear—of the Frontiersmen are shared with those of his Scouting movement. On the outbreak of hostilities in 1914, the Legion was offered to the Imperial War Office as a fighting unit, and the entourage of hunters, explorers, cowboys, colonialists, seal-poachers and mavericks who made up the 25th Battalion embarked from Plymouth to Mombasa, where they arrived on 4 May 1915. A later note written by Colonel H. R. Pownall about the personnel of the Legion in Hong Kong applies equally to the African contingent: "They are mostly, but not entirely, men of middle age—or older, who have 'knocked about' a good deal and like the glamour of a Stetson hat, boots and breeches, and a revolver holster, who, to their great credit, wish to have a useful function in emergency but are of too independent a spirit to stomach the bonds of army discipline in peace".[17]

Kearton—who admitted to being never a parade-ground soldier—was appointed together with Frederick C. Selous as Intelligence Officer, since "...I knew the country we were going to fight in and was a dead shot both with a rifle and with a revolver and something of an expert in rapid firing".[18] He is described in the Legion's records as "a brave and fearless leader in action, skilled in travelling unseen and unheard by the enemy".[19] Cherry remembered conditions in East Africa in his later autobiography *Adventures with Animals and Men*: "We were fighting 'open warfare' with a far-flung battle line. We had no continuous line of trenches and we never knew what unprotected piece of railway or exposed outpost would next be attacked in a sudden raid. We frequently marched without water, and were also short of rations. There was a lack of proper and adequate medical supplies and the danger of sudden and devastating outbreaks of fever and dysentery was always with us... More than anything else, the country was admirably suited for snipers and the native soldiers employed by the enemy were well trained in that section of the art of war".[20] Some of the tactics originated by the Frontiersmen in East Africa—for example, living off the land and replenishing food and ammunition supplies by night stealth raids on enemy camps—were later adopted by commando units.

While serving in East Africa, Cherry Kearton was seconded to the Royal Naval Air Service as a photographer, later working also for the Royal Flying Corps. Ada Kearton has described how "on one occasion Smuts sent for him personally to try and photograph a certain gun position that had remained undetected for twelve days. Within three hours Cherry had a well-defined picture of it".[21] He also shot and produced a private venture film, *Our Grip on the Huns in East Africa*, which was screened on the same bill as War Office productions in London. He returned to England—one of only sixty men, and the sole officer, surviving of the original contingent of 1,166 Frontiersmen—in 1919, with the rank of Captain, suffering from dysentery and malaria.

His lifestyle had left little time for his family, and as early as 1909 Cherry told his wife he was "weary of married life".[22] After he returned from the war, Mary applied unsuccessfully for the restoration of conjugal rights. Cherry arranged to be 'discovered' in a London hotel with another woman, and the couple were divorced on 20 April 1920. In 1921, Mary was married a second time, to the wealthy George M. Style, a citrus fruit grower who owned plantations in South Africa. They had a swallow-like existence, alternating their summer seasons between the Cape and England, where they had the choice of a house at Shelley Court, Tite Street, Chelsea, which had been Mary's home since 1915; a mansion in Kent; and a seaside villa owned by Style at Putsborough, Devon, which the Coates family had for long been renting for their summer holidays. Mary would die at Putsborough in 1940; George Style in 1946, of a bee sting, in Natal.

Cherry does not seem to have been close to his children, does not refer to them in his writing, and can have seen little of them when

Above: *Mary Kearton and Simba at the outspan, 1910.*

they were growing up. After the divorce there is no record of contact, and neither Edward Cherry nor Nina attended their father's funeral. He did however keep in touch with his nephews, Richard's sons, who would be his principal mourners, along with Cherry's second wife, Ada.

Ada Louisa Forrest was a professional singer, a soprano known as 'The Nightingale of Natal', who had studied under Sir Henry Wood, appeared at thirty-three Prom concerts in the years 1907–15, and performed with Sir Thomas Beecham. Born in Durban in 1877, she settled in London with her first husband, Allen Hawes, who died at the age of 55 in 1914. She was travelling on board the *Llanstephan Castle* to Cape Town in the autumn of 1920 to undertake a singing tour of South Africa when she met Cherry Kearton, and their paths were to cross a number of times over the following months. Cherry embarked on a "great trek from the Cape to Cairo" in May 1921, and on his return to London a year later, proposed to Ada Forrest. They were married at Marylebone on 14 April 1923. Ada "turned her back on the world of music",[23] and later adopted the name Ada Cherry Kearton, although the inscription on her tomb is Ada Forrest Kearton. They lived at first at Ada's residence at 30a Marlborough Hill, St Johns Wood; when Cherry's menagerie of exotic pets got too much for the small apartment, they moved in 1924 to the cottage they renovated

Above: 'The Jungle', Kenley, Surrey, c.1935.

of a former paper mill, which they renamed Great Ivy Mill, on the Loose Stream at Tovil, in Kent. They kept a flat in New Cavendish Street, London W1, in the early 1930s; while recuperating in hospital at Harrogate during this period, Cherry was shown an aerial photograph in which he recognised the garden and remains of the house in Firs Road, Kenley, where he had conducted his pioneering sound recordings in 1900. He subsequently bought the plot and built on it a house, The Jungle, where he and Ada lived from 1934.

Cherry and Ada travelled extensively together, for the most part in rather more comfort than had been the case in Cherry's earlier expeditions. They honeymooned in Algeria, Morocco, Egypt and the Sahara in 1923; safaried in East and South Africa in 1928; spent three months filming penguins on Dassen Island, off South Africa, in 1930; returned to Africa in 1933 and 1938; and were "fêted, cheered and entertained" in Indonesia, Australia and New Zealand in 1935–36.

The early films, shorts of a few minutes duration, were distributed by Charles Urban. On 30 September 1909, Cherry Kearton Limited was founded, with offices in Haymarket, to produce and distribute his own titles, specifically footage from the Roosevelt safari. Kearton bought the film company Warwick Trading Company for cash in 1912, and took over running the *Warwick Bioscope Chronicle* ("no matter where it happened, if it happened the Warwick got it"). At the same time he acquired rights in the lightweight Aeroscope camera, and filed a number of patents relating to cine cameras: one was for a simple lever operation to enable a camera to be set to take single, triple or continuous shots; another to minimise vibration. In 1914, the company offices were relocated to 117–119 Charing Cross Road, and a film factory and studio was opened at the former Chatham Club at Cramer Court, Clapham High Street. Beside nature films, Kearton produced a news chronicle, *The Whirlpool of War*, as well as comedies and dramas. Wartime commitments saw his business interests shut down in

Above: *Cherry Kearton and Togo, c.1935.*

November 1915, and Cherry Kearton Limited was formally wound up the following year. A later company, Cherry Kearton Films Ltd, with Cherry and Ada Kearton as directors, was founded in 1928.

Cherry Kearton suffered a heart attack on the steps of BBC Bush House during an air raid at the height of the Blitz on 27 September 1940, and died en route to St Mary's Hospital, Paddington. He had been giving a radio broadcast about Toto the tame gorilla on *Children's Hour*.

After Cherry's death, Ada retired to an apartment on Hampstead Way, NW11. She wrote two books: *Under African Skies*, a lively romance based on her experiences in Africa, which appeared in 1941, and an autobiography, *On Safari*, in 1956; she also edited, from earlier Cherry Kearton publications, *The Cherry Kearton Animal Book*, in 1958, and *Penguin Island*, in 1960. She appeared on *Desert Island Discs* on 8 October 1956, and was interviewed by Irene Slade for the BBC *I Remember* radio series in 1961. Towards the end of her life Ada returned to Surrey where she died in a nursing home at Woodcote, near Coulsdon, on 19 January 1966.

The cemetery of St Mary's Church, Caterham, is the burial place of Richard Kearton and his wife Ellen, and of Cherry Kearton and his wife Ada. Richard and Cherry's sister-in-law Frances is also buried here, as are Richard and Ellen's sons Richard and John, while the third son, Cherry, has a cremation plot; daughters Dora and Grace, and Grace's husband Howard Bentham, are buried at St Andrew, Kingswood.

There are two memorial tablets in Muker on the walls of what was the National School, where Richard and Cherry were educated; the school closed in 1979, and the building has traded in recent years as The Old School Craft Shop & Gallery. The inscription of the first reads: "In memory of Richard Kearton F.Z.S. Naturalist, Author and Lecturer". Paid for by public subscription, it was unveiled in June 1929 by Mr Burgoyne Johnston of Reeth, in a ceremony that included children's sports and a concert. A similar tablet, funded by Ada Kearton, reads: "In memory of Cherry Kearton. Naturalist, Author and Explorer. Pioneer of Wildlife Photography". When it was unveiled in 1943, the *Yorkshire Post* remarked that now "the world may dispose of the idea that Swaledale people had a greater affection for Richard than for Cherry".

In her will, Ada Kearton endowed the Cherry Kearton Medal & Award, bestowed on a discretionary annual basis by the Royal Geographical Society to "a traveller concerned with the study or practice of natural history, with a preference for those with an interest in nature photography, art or cinematography". The Medal was first awarded to Eric Hosking in 1968, and subsequent recipients include David Attenborough, Eric Ashby and Frans Lanting.

A number of the buildings associated with the Keartons suffered by wartime action. The Jungle, Kenley, which had been built on the site of a house burnt out by an aeroplane crash, was itself bombed shortly before Cherry's death in 1940. The Cassell factory and offices at La Belle Sauvage were destroyed by a fire bomb in 1941. William James Coates's home in Mill Hill received a direct hit from a V1 flying bomb, and the Coates's factory in Wood Street was razed to the ground during the Blitz. A tunnel, built by Richard under the garden of Ashdene as a shelter from Zeppelin raids in the First World War, was destroyed by a bomb in the Second.

The family home, Richard and Cherry's birthplace at Corner House, Thwaite, still stands, its lintels carved with birds by a later owner, John George Reynoldson, to commemorate the Keartons. Cherry and Ada's house at Tovil, Great Ivy Mill, survives intact. Ashdene passed into the hands of Frances Kearton, and on her death to her sister's daughter Marjorie Crerar; it was demolished in 1994, and a block of flats, Kearton Court, occupies the site. A housing development on the site of The Jungle is called Kearton Close.

Above: *Commemorative carvings, Corner House, Thwaite.*

Various Kearton artefacts are scattered among the nation's museums and libraries. In South Kensington, Richard Kearton's camera is in the Science Museum, while the Natural History Museum Library houses the Cherry Kearton Collection, a substantial archive of photographs, negatives and film taken in the 1920s and 1930s, donated to the Museum in 1990 by Dr Cherry Kearton, Richard Kearton's grandson. Patents registered in the years 1908–14 by Cherry Kearton for film cameras, projectors and a microphone are in the archive of the Patent Office. The British Film Institute has the most complete collection of commercially released films shot and produced by Cherry Kearton, donated by Ada. A portfolio of Kearton prints presented by Howard Bentham to the Nature Conservancy Board in the 1950s passed into the hands of the Royal Photographic Society, whose collection is now held by the National Media Museum in Bradford, which is also home to Cherry's film camera, bought at auction in 2013. It was announced in January 2016 that, due to lack of funding, the future of the National Media Museum is threatened, and parts of its collections, including the RPS portfolio and Cherry Kearton's camera, are to be consolidated in a new national photographic collection at the Victoria & Albert Museum, London. Less than a mile from the National Media Museum, the J. B. Priestley Library at the University of Bradford holds editions of most Kearton titles, together with the W. R. Mitchell Archive of correspondence and other Kearton-related material collected by Dr Mitchell when writing his book about the brothers, *Watch the Birdie!* The Dales Countryside Museum in Hawes has material relating to the Keartons, including a collection donated by Chester Murray in 2010, which formed the basis of a Kearton exhibition, 'Unexpected Photographic Adventures', mounted by the Museum in the summer of 2013.

CHAPTER TWO

The first nature photography book

The moment of "the genesis of natural history photography so far as the Kearton Brothers are concerned"[1] was remembered years later by both brothers as, appropriately enough, a flash, the blink of a shutter. They were staying with some Yorkshire friends near Enfield, Middlesex, when, on 10 April 1892, they took a walk across the fields. Cherry brought along his Kodak camera. According to the account given in 1926 by Richard, in his autobiography, *A Naturalist's Pilgrimage*, "I found the nest of a song thrush in a rather picturesque situation. I called out to Cherry: 'Here, come and let us see what sort of a fist you can make of this bird's nest with your old sun-picture apparatus'". The result so impressed Richard that he "at once determined to write a book on British birds' nests and illustrate it from beginning to end with photographs taken direct from nature".

The events were given a different slant in an interview with Cherry Kearton that appeared in the *Yorkshire Post*, 8 April 1931. According to this report, it was Cherry himself who found the thrush's nest, and "stuck the camera up, and started to focus" unprompted. And it was not Richard, but "my friend" who remarked: "That's the idea. Nobody has thought of it before", apparently reading in Cherry's mind the notion that this could be the start of something new—nature photography with "the idea of illustrating books".

Neither account got it quite right, according to Cherry's widow Ada Kearton who, writing sixty-four years after the event, added the plausible rider that only when studying the enlarged print, a week after the photograph had been taken, had the suggestion of producing a book first been voiced—by Richard.

Whoever had the idea—and however it would be remembered later—it was an extraordinary moment. The photograph in question has gone into the record books as the first ever taken of a bird's nest with eggs, a fortuitous result for what appears, at face value, to have been a casual snapshot. But what takes the breath away is the imaginative leap it inspired. The happy accident of a single shot is one

Left: *Song thrush's nest, Enfield. The first photograph of a bird's nest with eggs, 1892.*

matter: to project from it the commitment to an enterprise demanding numerous moments of equal good luck—which, on the face of it, would be required if Richard's vow to photographically document the nests of all British breeding birds were to be fulfilled—suggests a way of thinking that is at once go-getting, stubborn and foolhardy. And that, of course, was precisely what was needed. This would be the first systematic photographic catalogue of a natural taxonomy, perhaps the most methodical application of the camera since Edweard Muybridge, and certainly the most ambitious field photography project to date. It was a task that would take years to complete, resulting in another 'first'—a nature book illustrated throughout by photographs.

The Keartons were ahead of the game, though not unique. As early as 1868, Alexander Charles Kennedy's *Birds of Berkshire and Buckinghamshire* had been illustrated with four photographic prints, each hand-coloured, pasted in on card, varnished and interleaved with tissue. The images—of owl, hoopoe, hooded crow and black tern—were of stuffed specimens.[2] Two years later the first photo of a living wild animal, a European white stork, was taken by Charles A. Hewins.[3] 1888 saw the publication of J. C. Mansell-Pleydell's *Birds of Dorsetshire*, which included an illustration of mute swans at Abbotsbury, printed by plates made from a line-screen of a photographic print; while in the spring of the same year, Benjamin Wyles succeeded in photographing gulls in flight at Southport.[4] Closer to home, as far as the Keartons were concerned, the endeavours of R. B. Lodge of Enfield would lead to him taking credit in 1895 for the first photograph of a wild bird—a lapwing—on the nest; others, including Lodge's assistant O. G. Pike, were not far behind. But despite the camera's rapid growth in popularity during the 1890s—the end of the century saw "256 photographic clubs and an estimated four million camera owners in Britain"[5]—it was not until 1899 that the first forum, the Zoological Photographic Club, was founded, and even then "only a few naturalists, fired by the examples of Lodge and the Keartons, were beginning to realise what an enormous difference photography would make to natural history illustration".[6]

The ephemeral nature of their chosen subject, nests with eggs, meant they had to move fast when the time came. Success depended on being able to locate an example of the nest of any given species, identify it, and reach within a few feet of it with bulky photographic

Right: *Puffin's egg and burrow, Farne Islands.*

equipment. To complicate matters, this would have to be done at the right moment in the breeding season, and without causing distress to the parent birds. Each of the photographs they produced, on location and often in inaccessible or badly-lit situations, would need to show nest and eggs clearly enough for identification purposes, preferably with something of the characteristic surrounding habitat. And when all that had been done, they would have to attend to written descriptions of birds, nests and eggs that were detailed and accurate. The Kearton brothers would need, not least, to vouchsafe their authority and prove their credibility for the book to stand a chance of winning an audience; in some quarters in the late nineteenth century "photography was not yet seen as objective and needed additional evidence to testify to the validity of the results".[7]

They agreed from the start that Cherry would take the photographs, and Richard would write the text. The elder brother was already a published author, his first break having come in the late 1880s, when Cassell's editor Lewis Wright commissioned him to write the nest and egg part to Walter Swaysland's *Familiar Wild Birds*, published as a partwork. It was so well received that the publisher undertook to reissue it in 1890 as a stand-alone volume under the title *Birds' Nests, Eggs and Egg Collecting*. This was the only Kearton edition without photographs, the illustrations being coloured gravure plates by Alexander Francis Lydon, the engraver and watercolourist who had previously illustrated *The Natural History of Nests and Eggs of British Birds*, by the Revd Francis Orpen Morris. On publication, Kearton sold the rights, receiving in total royalties of three guineas, for a book that over the next thirty years went through two editions and nineteen reprints, causing him later to lament that "I have out-Miltoned Milton".[8] (His standing regret at the profits of authorship was reported in the *Yorkshire Post*, 13 April 1925, when he calculated that despite all of his books having been successful in selling up to seven or eight editions, "I have taken less out of them per hour for time expended than anybody else who has touched them, whether compositor, block-maker, machine-minder, bookbinder, or the man who has sold them over a counter".) The red cloth binding of the first edition was shortly substituted for a practical drab green, a model for most of Richard Kearton's subsequent publications, all of which appeared under the imprint of his old firm, Cassell.

The research Richard had undertaken for *Birds' Nests, Eggs, and Egg Collecting* would stand him in good stead for the new volume. Despite

Left: *Jay's nest and eggs.*

later protestations that he had "never been anything in the nature of a literary stylist",[9] he had by this time completed a copy writing apprenticeship, knew to borrow a little from the erudite atmosphere at Ludgate Hill, and mixed acute observation and occasional wordy jocularity into his fluent journalism. (It may be refreshing to compare Kearton's reportage with the tendency of modern nature writers to use deliberately supercharged vocabulary and syntax to demand that our relationship with nature be a poetic one, and to impose a sense of awe; one can't help regretting that the effect of this is sometimes the opposite of connecting us to nature). Kearton's publications included wildlife contributions to a number of in-house periodicals such as *Live Stock Journal* and *Little Folks Magazine*, and several pieces for *The Speaker*, one being titled 'The Soul of a Poacher's Dog'. But knowledge-able naturalists able to write are not a rare breed; arguably, what sustained Richard Kearton, as much as the bird-wisdom gleaned on fell and moor, and writerly skills cultivated in London EC4, was a shrewdness tuned over years of putting images and text together at his desk-job in the publicity department of Cassell: to appeal directly to the imagination of the public, and jump on any opportunity.

For his part, Cherry had some experience as amateur photogra-pher, having bought his first camera a few years earlier at the age of eighteen or nineteen, from a shop in Fleet Street. He does not identify make or model, but his description of a "small hand camera, made of bright metal", the detail of the outfit including two plates "in black rubber bags",[10] and the remarkably cheap retail price of five shillings, all point to the Demon Detective Camera. Introduced in 1889, this was a stylish, futuristic sculptural object, with its clean lines and bright nickel plating. It is easy to see the attraction for the young Cherry Kearton, who would later proudly recall a remark made by a colleague on the daily commuter train into London: "Kearton, you'll always be twenty-five years before your time".[11]

Despite the camera's stamped back proclaiming it "The Wonder of the World", and the seemingly prophetic advert that boasted "No movement is too rapid for it—the racehorse at greatest speed, the flight of birds, even the lightning flash itself", the camera with its crude elastic-band powered mechanism would have been of little use for nature photography. Indeed, Cherry enjoyed such slight success in securing photographs of anything, moving or static, that he "nearly abandoned photography for ever".[12] But in 1889 he was unable to resist the bargain of a guinea box camera, an Eastman Kodak, which one of his work colleagues was selling second-hand for 14 shillings, and shortly "began to perpetrate all sorts of weird atrocities in

Above: *"Our Outfit"*.

portraiture and landscape photography".[13] This was the camera he used on the song thrush's nest at Enfield.

The first Kodak celluloid film camera had arrived in 1888, and with it the age of the snapshot. This had the effect of establishing the distinction between amateur and expert photography, while normalising the acceptance of the photograph as an evidential tool. Forward-looking—not yet universal—orthodoxy was beginning to insist that if you wanted to know what a thing looked like, a photographic study with its guarantee of fidelity was at least as good as the real thing.

Such plausibility could only be won using something more than a box camera; after some experimentation the Keartons settled on a Dallmeyer half-plate camera with nine-inch rectilinear lens. It was fitted with a near-silent roller-blind type shutter made by Thornton & Pickard, and operated pneumatically. This was pretty much a studio camera; for greater versatility in the field, when photographing moving or restless subjects, Cherry made a characteristically ingenious adaptation. He mounted an adjustable miniature camera on top, which was focussed "exactly like its working companion beneath" and racked out simultaneously when the focussing screw on the larger machine was turned. The miniature was then used not for taking the photograph itself, but "as a sort of view-finder", the shutter on the plate camera being released when "a sufficiently clear and strong definition of his object [is seen] upon the ground-glass of the miniature camera".[14]

The Keartons were nothing if not canny, and must have known that their timing could hardly have been bettered. Whether or not it was true of their endeavour that, as Cherry reported, "nobody had thought of it before", the fact was that it had not long been possible. The development of field photography had hitherto been hampered by its reliance on the wet collodion plate, which suffered the handicap of having to be developed within a very short period after exposure. But by 1892, the alternative was commonplace of the dry-gel paper plate, which was not only twenty times as sensitive to light, but remained 'live' long enough for plates exposed in the field to be taken back to the darkroom for development several hours later. Even this was not always practical in the circumstances, and the Keartons recalled improvising 'darkrooms' beneath a blanket or under the bed of a boarding house. Their expeditions were necessarily encumbered not only with the weighty camera and tripod, but bottles of developing chemicals, papier mâché trays and stocks of plates. (As an indication of the burden on the field photographer at the time, the Keartons' contemporary R. B. Lodge and his brother George "used to tramp miles across rough country pushing a huge 12 in. x 10 in. plate camera on a wheelbarrow").[15]

Another advance that made the Keartons' quest newly possible was in the printing process, which they experienced at first hand at La Belle Sauvage. The commonest method of printing illustrations

Right: *Cherry Kearton photographing a shag, Shetland.*

had been until recently—as with Richard Kearton's first book—gravure, whose advantage of a broad tonal range is outweighed by its expense, making it best suited to long print runs. But the development in the 1880s of the half-tone process, which reduced grey scales to a grid of variable size dots, enabled the mechanical transfer of photographic image onto letterpress block. As they were printed in exactly the same way, metal type and mounted block could now be locked up together, text and image mixing and mingling on the page in the modern newspaper style. The compromise was that to achieve quality reproduction of the images, the stock had to be an unabsorbent, glossy coated art paper, whose harsh contrast was less sympathetic to the reading of text. Half-tone printing was not only much cheaper than gravure, permitting for the first time low-priced editions of heavily illustrated books, but had a grainy reality that was persuasive of a new aesthetic of immediate contact with the physical world. Not for nothing would the Keartons proclaim their photographs as having been taken "direct from nature"; the directness being both proximate and temporal.

They started locally, acquiring the weekday habit of rising at 4:30 a.m. to scour trees, hedges, outhouses and eaves for nest-building birds, before catching the train to London, where they were at Ludgate Hill by nine o'clock. A 'field alert', surely one of the first ever, was set up, with dependable birdwatchers, landowners, farmers and gamekeepers primed to telegram the brothers at work with any promising sighting of a nest or nesting bird. To waste an hour of daylight was to miss an opportunity that might not recur until the following year, if at all.

This diligence would have sufficed for many of the common and less common species to be found around the home counties. But each species on the list of British breeding birds, around 183 in all, has its own unique distribution map, whose boundaries are set by a complex of factors: latitude, diet, habit, availability of nesting sites, predation, and so on. Some migrants breed close to their point of landfall, be it East Anglian wetland or Scottish island. Those whose numbers have been reduced by persecution are most likely to cling on in the least populated locations, and to build their nests in the least humanly accessible sites. The habitat and nesting place of each bird on the list—cliff or crag, marsh or moor—would present its own challenge.

And so the breeding seasons of the years 1892–95 became marathons of travelling, finding and photographing. Weekends were

Left: *"Oystercatcher at home"*.

intense with photography on location, usually reached by train and thence horse cab or foot. Annual leave, taken during the critical months of April, May and June, gave the brothers time to reach some of the more extreme locations: Achnacarry, Lochaber, for the nest of the osprey; Mull, for white-tailed and golden eagles; Bass Rock, for gannets; Ailsa Craig, for puffin; the Farne islands for eider and shelduck, as well as sandwich, arctic and common tern; the Saltees for cormorants, guillemots and kittiwakes; North Uist, for corncrakes; and Unst, in Shetland, for bonxies.

In their collation of examples of the nesting places of all British breeding birds, the Keartons were inadvertently making a survey of habitat and thus of issues of land ownership, stewardship and common rights of access. The acknowledgements in their early books are largely made to the landowners—peers of the realm, colonels and clergy prominent among them—who gave permission for the Keartons to be on their land, and to "the numerous factors, farmers, keepers, and boatmen" who assisted them.[16] In this area, as with conservation, attitudes were on the move; the significance being that the ultimate effect of the success of the Kearton project—an increase in birdwatching—coincided with the opening up of the countryside. The Commons Preservation Society had been founded in 1865 with the purpose of the salvation of common land; after amalgamating with the National Footpaths Preservation Society in 1899 to form the Open Spaces Society, the remit was broadened to include protecting and adding to the rights-of-way network in England and Wales, and later to campaigning for the inclusion of footpaths on Ordnance Survey maps. Individual interests in rambling were being consolidated in clubs that were likewise devoted to maintaining rights of way locally and regionally; a turning point in public awareness would later be achieved with the historic mass trespass of Kinder in 1932. Legislation remained somewhat behind the curve, with an Access to Mountains Bill introduced—and failing—for the first time in Parliament in 1884. Rights of way were extended in the Local Government Act of 1894 and the Law of Property Act of 1925, which opened to the public "for air and exercise" all commons in urban areas in England and Wales; but it would not be until a century after the Keartons that the Countryside & Rights of Way Act, 2000, would allow the conditional right to roam, principally on downs, moors, heaths and coastal land in England and Wales.

The other face of the new countryside awareness was habitat protection. The National Trust for Places of Historic Interest and Natural Beauty was incorporated in 1895; better known now for its

Above: *"Preparing to descend a cliff"*, Unst.

portfolio of country houses, the National Trust is concerned as much with protecting open spaces "for the preservation of their natural aspect, features and animal and plant life", and is currently responsible for the guardianship of 775 miles of coastline. Its first nature reserve was the enchanting Wicken Fen, acquired in 1899; the RSPB's own first nature reserve, Cheyne Court, Romney Marsh, would be secured in 1930. Post war, the National Parks and Access to the Countryside Act of 1949 identified both national parks and Areas of Outstanding Natural Beauty, while national nature reserves became recognised in the Wildlife and Countryside Act of 1981.

The hindrance of having to apply for written permission to access private land was nothing to what the Keartons would endure on location. Cherry Kearton, who would be responsible for getting the camera into some nigh-on impossibly tricky positions, prepared for the physical demands of the task with almost military rigour. He "underwent a training in swimming, long distance running, wrestling, boxing, and gymnastics, and holds, besides many other trophies, the National Physical Society's bronze medal and diploma for physical proficiency".[17] He learned ropework in Ireland from Mr John Usher, and was shortly descending sea cliffs hundreds of feet in height in pursuance of the nests and eggs of fulmar, kittiwake, gannet and shag. Richard, less physically able, was spared the most

Above: "Photographing a kingfisher's nesting hole in a river's bank".

extreme abseiling, but his picturesque account of what the brothers shared to achieve their goal shows that neither escaped discomfort:

> "We worked hard and honestly, sparing no pains, danger or expense in procuring what we considered interesting or instructive. For nights together we slept in empty houses and old ruins, descended beetling cliffs, swam to isolated rocks, waded rivers and bogs, and climbed lofty trees. We lay in wet heather for hours at a stretch, tramped many weary miles in the dark, and spent nights in the open air on lonely islands and solitary moors. On other occasions we have endured the pangs of hunger and thirst, and the torturing stings of insects, waited for days and days together for a single picture, and been nearly drowned, both figuratively and literally".[18]

The book appeared in 1895 under the title *British Birds' Nests: How, Where and When to Find and Identify Them*. The "adequate and instructive" descriptions of the materials of the nests are picked out by Richard Bowdler Sharpe, curator of the bird collection at the British Museum, South Kensington (now Natural History Museum), in his introduction as "most useful". These descriptions, whose authority was the first test of the book's claim to validity, were as Richard Kearton acknowledged drawn on the observations of the best naturalists of the day, including Morris, Swaysland, Montagu, Henry Seebohm and others; but they are lightly touched also with the authenticity of Kearton's own experience, observations such as that for the grasshopper warbler, "the position of the nest and the skulking, mouse-like habits of its owner, making it very hard to find", ringing true. Kearton would maintain a lifelong interest in the construction and materials of birds' nests, classifying nests into "roughly six separate classes: 1. open-topped nests, 2. covered nests, 3. nests in tunnels purposely dug for them, 4. nests in natural holes, 5. nests covered over by birds when leaving voluntarily, 6. nests that are not nests at all in the true sense of the word". He went on to demonstrate the symbiotic correlations of structure, materials, colour and number of eggs, against their owners' ability to defend, whether in pairs or in colonies.[19]

But it was the photography that provoked Dr Sharpe to express his opinion that this, the first nature book illustrated throughout by photography, "marked a new era in natural history". It did so, in part, by the Keartons establishing at this early stage the ground rules for nature photography. Its enduring appeal would lie, they showed, in its complex function as a compromise of intentions: documentary, to illustrate some truth in the appearance or behaviour of the subject, as aid to recognition and knowledge, essentially a frozen record of what we might see with our own eyes under the most favourable conditions; revelatory, of some insight of the photographer, essentially what the superior skills and experience of the photographer, and the superior optical characteristics of his equipment, enable us to see that we cannot have seen before; and pictorial, to create an image that is appealing—or dramatic or beautiful—of itself, irrespective of the subject matter, essentially marking the distinction between seeing the order nature creates for itself, and the formality of a human inter-pretation of nature. Any good wildlife photograph will demonstrate one or more of these virtues. The balance of them is in some ways a measure of the character and intention of the photographer.

The photographs impress, at first glance, as good documentary images at least. So much would be expected. But it is only when we read Richard's notes that we learn that the Keartons were prepared to compromise the veracity of appearance for the sake of artistry. Many nests are, for very obvious reasons, hidden to some extent, typically by being built within a screen of foliage. Often they are in shadowy locations, both for concealment and to protect the eggs from the direct heat of the sun. So to get what they wanted, the Keartons were obliged to undertake some degree of 'gardening', folding back stems and leaves to expose the nest, and where necessary illuminating it with flashlight; in a handful of cases, including wheatear, swallow and starling, they went so far as to move the nest into daylight. In so doing, they created pictorial—if not picturesque—images that often centre the nest and eggs within a coronet of foliage, still lifes that call to mind the cornucopias of a harvest festival. These are quite Victorian images of decorative abundance, in which nature is revealed as simultaneously bounteous and contained within human boundaries of elegance and design. Forty years on from the heyday of the prolific William Henry 'Birds Nest' Hunt, who painted nature scenes from studio dioramas with unrealistically prominent nests, the Keartons could return art to nature.

Their choice of equipment and up-close techniques caused them difficulties in controlling depth of field, a problem compounded when it came to live subjects that demanded fast shutter speeds. Under favourable conditions, the subject could be isolated against a diffuse background (see for example Kingfisher, p.104). Equally, surroundings could be brought into the picture when it benefited to show, for example, a nest's location and prevailing vegetation (e.g. Corncrake, p.54). But often, when a good subject shot was compromised by a fuzzy background, an artist was called in to lend form where there had been none to shrub or sky, using pen and brush to add, for instance, unsubtle outlines to foliage around a nightingale (see p.128). The animals, birds and nests themselves were not, and would never have been, modified in this way, but touching up did rescue from the picture editor's bin some charmingly oblique shots, such as a general coastal landscape titled "The nesting place of the common buzzard and the peregrine falcon", and the seemingly arbitrary "Surrey cottage under the tiles of which a numerous colony of swifts breed yearly".

There is one other consideration to take into account regarding the aesthetic of the Keartons' early photographic work. Not only did they improve on what they found by gardening, and by varying the light conditions; their subject matter at this stage was static, disinhibiting restrictions on length of exposure. All of these conditions conspired to iron out particularities, the image selected for publication being the one closest to the archetype. So what we notice, in browsing their book, is a sense in their most careful studies of super-reality, of the photograph being not of nature as found but its epitome, in much

Right: *Blue tit's nest in a hollow fruit tree. "The entrance to the nest was in the centre of a decayed branch... the hole through which the eggs are to be seen, being cut artificially through the wood, so as to show its exact position".*

the way that a portrait painter or figure sculptor is able to stylise his or her subject. This, coincidentally or not, reflects the changing perception of photographs in this era, those in the 1890s being seen as "trophies or aesthetic objects" while by the early twentieth century they were "in the process of becoming disciplinary objects", e.g. records of bird life and behaviour;[20] we might note the equivalent movement towards naturalism in social photography in the same period, away from the posed group and fixed expression. Cecil Beaton was perhaps more prescient than he knew when he described the photographic work of the Keartons as "*monuments* [my italics] of extraordinary patience and tenacity".[21]

Of the 183 species described in the Keartons' first book, 124 are illustrated in full page or half page plates. It was no doubt a disappointment that the original goal of illustrating all subjects could not be fulfilled, and in his introduction Richard wrote an appeal for the whereabouts of nests of any outstanding species. The search continued, resulting in the 1899 publication of *Our Rarer British Breeding Birds: Their Nests, Eggs and Summer Haunts*, an opportunity to illustrate a further 56 species, a few of which had been treated with general illustrations in the original volume. The title of the new book was, in fact, somewhat misleading: the types covered were not necessarily "rarer", but simply a round-up of most of those that had evaded inclusion in the earlier volume, including such relatively commonplace types as nuthatch and jay.

In 1907, the mission initiated fifteen years earlier was finally achieved when the best of the contents of the two books, detailing almost all of the regular British breeding birds, was combined with fifteen colour plates of specimen egg collections for identification purposes, Rembrandt gravure plates and other new material, in a substantial, if rather busy, new volume, which was issued as a revised and enlarged edition of the original title. *British Birds' Nests*, in its final form, was the largest single project undertaken by the Keartons working as a team.

But by this time their reputation was already sealed; it had been the first edition of 1895 that announced their arrival as heavyweights in the arena of nature photography. The three years' work leading to its publication was of such intensity, and so broad ranging, to make them the most experienced in their field, their credibility and authority being shortly recognised in Richard's acceptance as Fellow of the Zoological Society.

Left: *Corncrake's nest and eggs, North Uist.*

CHAPTER THREE

The Kearton partnership

"I can see them now... passing along a woodland path on the way to the pool, the tall athletic figure of my Uncle Cherry, in dark-green tweeds and cap, striding ahead eager to get to the scene of operations, a brilliant, wayward, magnetic personality. My father, Richard, who was partly crippled, plodding along behind, the indomitable and infinitely resourceful originator of nature photography and most of the methods since used in its pursuit."—from *Nature Memories*, by John Kearton

The Kearton partnership was from the start an informal agreement, initiated seemingly spontaneously in 1892. Its original purpose was to see the publication of one volume, *British Birds' Nests*; in the event, the active collaboration lasted off and on for around sixteen years. Besides still photography and books, the years of the partnership saw work produced in the media of film and sound recording. The last record in Richard's diaries of the brothers working together in the field dates from June 1908, when they "got a good lot of film of Songthrush, a bit of Wheatear and a bit of Butcher birds".[1] After this, the 'Richard & Cherry Kearton' brand name continued to appear on books and films written and edited by Richard, Cherry's contributions being taken from stock, or shot on solo outings.

They were of course not only partners, but brothers and friends. In print, Richard was never less than generous in his estimation of the younger sibling with "the love of adventure in his blood" and "never-failing sense of humour in positions of danger and disappointment", revelling in the phenomenal good luck that blessed him "while engaged in all kinds of perilous work".[2] The tales of how Cherry narrowly missed death from rock-falls, landslides, drowning, poisonous snakes and charging animals; how he was prevented by business from taking the berth he had booked on the *Titanic*, and by officiousness from travelling in the USA on a train that was wrecked in a wash-out, were rehearsed and polished over time, giving colour

Left: *"Method of photographing birds' nests situated in high hedges".*

to the books and lectures of both Keartons, and veracity to end results wrested against the odds.

Cherry, aided by a hearty stoicism and lashings of the recurrent trait of his ancestors identified by Richard Kearton as "picturesque rashness",[3] grew into the character created by his own anecdotes: a bluff, witty raconteur whose ruggedness and masculinity belonged to the boys' action hero. A type familiar from the adventure writing of John Buchan, or perhaps more precisely Rider Haggard's Allan Quartermain, whose colonial values were based on a real-life later acquaintance, the adventurer and giant of the African safari F. C. Selous. If this paints him as something of a dyed-in-the-wool figure, it's worth noting that he loved modernity, its promise of greater comforts and opportunities, invested in the latest equipment and was given to occasional prophecies such as "the book of the future will speak, or rather sing, for itself..."[4] Some of the most important decisions of Cherry's life appear to have been made impetuously, including his determination to go to Africa and, later, the Antipodes, and spur-of-the-moment resolutions to purchase houses at Tovil and Kenley. "Exasperating and lovable", Kearton was as doggedly and demonstrably loyal and generous to his acquaintances as he was punctilious in his duty to chastise whoever fell short of expectations. Richard found him possessed of a mixture of "nerve and nervousness",[5] fearless in the face of real danger and fussing over petty discomforts. His outward assurance was not matched by his introspection, and out of his peculiarly adrenalin-blanketed comfort zone he could swing between sentimentality and coming over as fickle and petulant, a practical joker who doesn't know when to stop, a showman happiest when stealing the show, immodest enough to describe "not the least amusing thing [in my house], as many people have assured me—myself, with a pretty large repertoire of stories collected in my travels around the world".[6] One of those stories told of a taxi driver in Australia who on learning the identity of his distinguished fare was so overwhelmed by awe that he crashed into the kerb.[7]

As to what Cherry thought of himself, it is hard to avoid the suspicion that the chapter-long dedication to Captain Cook prefacing the account of Kearton's final overseas voyage, *I Visit the Antipodes*, is meant to show how uncannily alike are Captain Kearton and Captain Cook. The parallels begin with Kearton's discovery that, "strangely enough", he was born in a Yorkshire village less than fifty miles from Cook's birthplace, and conclude with this character assessment: "[He], a splendid giant of a man with an iron constitution, was at heart a

Above: *"Where Kittiwakes breed", Noup of Noss.*

simple, kindly fellow, who lived strictly and vigorously, and this… helped to equip him for those arduous enterprises which his bold and penetrating genius, his indefatigable application, and undeviating perseverance, eminently qualified him to undertake".[8]

It would be interesting to know more of what Cherry thought of Richard, but while allowing that "our partnership was most happy and successful",[9] in his books he rarely attempted to get under the skin of those around him, and made no exception in the case of his partner and brother. Some of Richard's personality we can take almost as read: the patience and perseverance that were so funda-

Above: *"Robin's nest in a nosebag"*.

mental to his calling, whose successes owe much also to his energy, ingenuity and self-belief. Unlike Cherry, he was at times rather Luddite, deploring noisy machinery, sceptical about the future of the motor car and, surprisingly, cinema, writing in a letter to Frank Lowe in 1925: "Moving pictures of any sort have had their day".[10] Richard was staunch in his earning, generous in his giving and cautious in his spending. He had a sharp eye for character, mentally sorting the human wheat from the chaff as he went, and despairing of all folly. He was an inspiration to his children, an educator who believed in "teaching through the eye",[11] an enthusiastic and witty man with a big laugh, who saw it a virtue to appear an everyman, equally at home mixing with writers and politicians or milking a countrywoman's cow; he would end a lecture at a prison by saluting the prisoners; greet an Irishman with "to be sure begorrah". Richard had little time for pomp, and would wear his field tweeds to even the most formal social event, ready to answer the alert of a rare sighting. His egalitarianism is illustrated in this bijou parable:

> "One day I was walking across an estate in my neighbourhood, and was met by a stranger who asked: 'To whom does this place belong?' 'To me', I replied. I suppose my sunbleached green tweed jacket and rough, muddy boots filled him with worldly incredulity, for he exclaimed: 'Indeed! I thought it was owned by Sir So-and-So'. 'Yes', I answered, 'he is the nominal owner, and takes the rent and the trouble, but I get all the pleasure out of the place and count that the real test of ownership'".[12]

Until the outbreak of the First World War, Richard habitually took a field study break every year during the nesting season, setting out in mid to late May and returning home usually around the start of July. Trips to Norway, Holland, North Uist, the Shetlands and the Cairngorms were interspersed with visits to Swaledale and Cumbria, where he was put up by family members. While staying with his uncle John at Nateby, he recorded "notes on bird songs" in his nature diary for 7 June 1900. At 8 o'clock the birds singing were lark, thrush, blackbird, garden warbler, willow warbler, chaffinch, and meadow pipit. At 8.20 he heard a wren, at 8.30 a linnet, and so on. Eventually "I sat down under a wall and called a cuckoo to me. He flew round and round, alighted, called, barked and swore at me in the most frightful fashion and would not go away. Every time I called he stopped to listen and then went on".[13]

What is singular is that on this day, while Richard was marking off the hours and minutes in bird song, his brother, companion and professional partner, Cherry, was married at Godstone Church, Surrey, to Mary Burwood Coates. Given the closeness of the two brothers, this might be read as indicative of some rift. There is, however, no evidence to support this; in fact, in his diaries Richard's sole dissenting comment came as late as June 1913, when having lost two days of "beautiful light and my best photographic time" preparing photos for his brother's book, Richard wondered of Cherry "if he would have done as much for me without a great deal of grousing".[14] The more plausible interpretation is that for Richard, social ceremony would always come a sorry second to nature and to work.

Above: *"Daisies Asleep (photographed before sunrise); Daisies Awake (after sunrise)"*.

> "[Cherry] took, in those early years, pictures which have never been surpassed for clarity, dramatic composition and complete naturalness; and he took them without the trip-wires, telephoto and wide-angle lenses, and the hundred-and-one other aids which are now at a photographer's disposal."
> —Ada Cherry Kearton, *On Safari* p.49.

Our idea of 'the Keartons'—their identity, their brilliant advances, and the greater part of the work for which they are now remembered—belongs largely to the years of their active partnership. During this time they developed most of their sustaining techniques; experimented most broadly, and produced some of their best and most imaginative work. There were particular circumstances that mitigated the subject matter of their photographs: the difficulties surrounding the photography of birds in the wild (see Chapter 4) were central to this period of work, and the years spent developing solutions to those problems, which to less resourceful minds might have felt a time of frustration, were grasped by the Keartons as an opportunity to widen their remit.

The results appeared in three of their early books. *With Nature and*

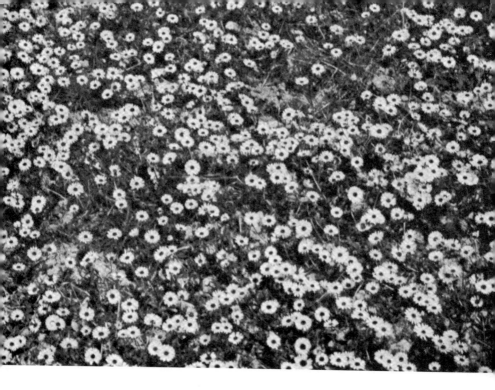

a Camera was published in 1897; *Wild Life at Home* the following year; and *Wild Nature's Ways* in 1903. Within the covers of these ostensibly 'bird' titles the Keartons paraded a range of animals and insects; showed us some of their methods of working; delved into the lore and customs of country people they had met on their travels; and published several incidental plates unique in their nature.

Some of these, perhaps the Keartons' most compelling photographs of this period, seem to straddle the boundary between 'the two natures', the one inviolable, the other negotiable (these are discussed below in Chapter 7). In so doing they reveal aspects of wild nature to have a cultural pattern. For example, Richard Kearton took a number of comparative pairings of patches of wild flowers with the camera pointing vertically downward, effectively flattening the topography and homogenising the light to create a semblance of artificial pattern, like a scattershot Voysey wallpaper. We may not expect photographs of daisies to surprise us, to make us 'see' daisies for the first time; but Kearton's lantern slides of 'Daisies Asleep' and 'Daisies Awake',[15] a photographic pair taken 'near to London, before the sun had risen and afterwards', did take many daisypicking countryfolk by surprise. This was due less perhaps to the mundane observation that daisies close their petals at night, than to the sudden, magical transformation displayed in the two plates. The photographs are crammed with the single phenomenon, so that however uninspiring as a fact, it has suddenly become, in this early 'before-and-after', unforgettable as an image. The photos repeat a fundamental organic property in displaying both symmetry and asymmetry, so that we instinctively compare and contrast them. There is both a pattern—each plant demanding more or less equal space, and their flowers growing into the least-crowded, brightest positions—and a random element, which also strikes a chord in our evolutionary instincts. (The stochastic process, in which events are scattered in a partially random manner like arrows on a target, is believed to be conditional for genetic change). We seem to recognise that these images portray a fundamental truth before we realise what it is: this is Kearton's "teaching through the eye" in action, the learning process filling a discernible gap between the visual impact of the image and the cognition of its subject, like the pause between the punchline and the laughter. And the two photographs might be an object lesson in some principles of photography: the record; the selected composition; abstract form; the series; and the scientific.

As remarkable was the photograph taken from the stuffed ox beside a water hole, showing a song thrush that, "after sipping at the muddy water very leisurely for a while, hopped on to a flint, which formed a sort of miniature island in the pond, and stood with drooping wings, contemplating a bath".[16] Kearton "made a slight noise in order to induce her to listen" before taking a shot, framed to include the body of the bird on the rock, the reflection in the water, and the shadow on the surface. The plate, published with the caption "Substance, shadow and reflection", is an early and striking forerunner of the modern 'knowing' nature photograph, which simultaneously documents a subject and its location, reveals and demonstrates some natural phenomenon, and expresses an aspect of the photographer's insight. Such a complexity, in aspiring to— perhaps fulfilling—the condition of art, achieves what is sometimes termed 'epiphany', in this context a revelation of the wondrous in art; here it applies, not only to a certain sacred symbolism in the trinity of images begotten, as it were, by the divinity of light, but also one might contend to the Keartons' sudden knowing of their art in this image. For it at once celebrates that the true and only subject of the photographer's art is light, its transmission and translation; and at the same time alerts us to another trinity, of the optical events that

Right: *"Song thrush. Substance, shadow and reflection".*

Above: *"Primroses photographed in first moments of the twentieth century"*.

contribute to the revelation of the photograph: the visual presence of the subject itself; the act of recording that subject; and finally the act of looking at the photographic image. The photographer, we acknowledge, is essentially a physicist, dealing in optical properties; and also a metaphysician, responsible for illuminating us with the nature of things.

One other photograph that belongs in this grouping was taken as a team effort by Richard, his brother Cherry and daughter Grace. In Richard's words: "The closing days of the nineteenth century were so mild that primroses were in bloom in many woods throughout the south of England. Wishing to celebrate the commencement of the new century by some photographic exploit, we got a root of these flowers under focus during the last evening of the old one, put a plate into the camera, charged our magnesium flash-lamp with powder, and waited for the last stroke of midnight to boom from a neighbouring church steeple. Directly that happened, we fired, and secured the foregoing record during the first moment of the twentieth century".[17] Here the value of the photograph in documenting nature is stripped away, and with it the significance of the flower as a product of nature; the primrose becomes purely symbolic, potent with the cultural significance bestowed on it by the photographer, which transforms it alchemically from a signifier of botany to one of time.

Now this is truly revolutionary. Within eight years of their first use of a camera, the Keartons had in a way subverted the nature of photography. At a moment when the whole country must have been ringing with celebration, and any number of 'photo-opportunities' for recording the historic moment would have presented themselves, they took a charming but rather ordinary photograph of a not exceptional clump of flowers. Why this should be subversive is simply that the camera had become an honorary overseer of the virtue of truth—'the camera never lies'. And this photograph throws back the onus of veracity onto its audience—it is a remarkable picture *if we choose to believe it*. We want to trust the photographer but we're sceptical of blind faith. We are made to acknowledge that the photograph, as the record of an event, is a condition of the photographer's integrity. Either it is light reflected from nineteenth-century primroses, exposed on a photographic plate, a nanosecond later, in the twentieth-century; or else it is nothing much.

One of the Keartons' most popular books, *With Nature and a Camera*, has perhaps the broadest scope of curiosity of all, including a lengthy section on their inspirational 1896 expedition to the remote Scottish island group of St Kilda. Here the Keartons were no less fascinated by the wildlife than by the anachronistic habits and customs of the isolated community, which was then becoming something of a freak show for day trippers from Oban. The book includes early examples of what would become a Kearton stock-in-trade, the photographic comparison: of the dress of married and unmarried St Kildan women; the author's ankle with a St Kildan ankle; the mainland wren with the St Kilda wren. There is a staged shot of a launching of the idiosyncratic St Kilda mailboat (a slight evolution of the message in a bottle); and cataloguing of local patterns of handcrafted doorlocks, lamps and brooches. There are some quite outstanding studies of the locals harvesting, with wire nooses on long rods, their staple food: puffin and fulmar. The same book features folk-studies of rustic occupations in other outposts: grouse netting and shooting; decoy men; gamekeepers; and a dramatic composition of two bird catchers, preserving their anonymity by looking out across the South Downs with their backs to the camera, the nets and other paraphernalia of their trade hung over their shoulders. These images may appear at first sight to belong to a nostalgic genre category; but they are studies of occupation, not character, and the observations are as detached as those of an anthropologist. After the Kearton partnership was wound up Richard would not pursue this type of photography; Cherry would, in Africa, with mixed results.

One reason the Keartons' records are so invaluable is that they documented their own techniques as meticulously as their subject matter. In the Introduction to their first book, Richard Bowdler Sharpe had expressed the opinion that "naturalists would especially like to hear more of their birds-nesting experiences in detail",[18] and after its publication, Richard Kearton had received a number of requests to be let in on the secrets of the Keartons' methods of working. He did so, candidly and generously. One can only wonder how many readers were tempted to follow the Keartons abseiling with their cameras and tripods down almost vertical cliffs hundreds of feet high, on ropes wound round stakes hammered into the rock; to extend the legs of their tripods with canes, and operate the camera by standing on the shoulders of an assistant; or to occupy hides fashioned from local materials, animal, vegetable or mineral. Even less probable was the widespread uptake of the use of a long ladder to steady the camera in a tall tree:

> "Occasionally some rare object, such as the nest of a siskin, built right away along the slender branch of a tall tree, cannot possibly be portrayed except from the top of a tall ladder, reared into a perfectly perpendicular position, and secured by means of strong guide ropes tied to surrounding trees. My brother has made studies from the very top of one of the tallest ladders in Britain so fixed, and testifies to the exhilarating qualities of the ordeal."[19]

At times, Richard's description of his brother's working practice turns from testimony to sheer admiration: "In a big tree with a multitude of branches I once saw him fix his camera, and, climbing above it in order to obtain a free space in which to work, focus and make his exposures whilst hanging absolutely upside down by the heels from a strong bough shooting out horizontally at some height above the apparatus".[20]

These techniques are illustrated in compositions of workshop-manual clarity: it is surely the mentality of the advertising manager at work here, making sure the message gets home. We see the attitude of the photographer; the deployment of his equipment; the conditions of his surroundings and, where appropriate, the location of his subject. All this may be read at a glance; all extraneous matter is relegated to the background. There are no dark arts in the way the Keartons obtained their pictures, and they appeared evangelical in their mission to inform and instruct others in their craft. As the one-time President of the Zoological Photographic Club, Riley Fortune, wrote of Richard Kearton in *The Naturalist*: "He was always ready in the kindest manner to help his fellow naturalists and photographers;

Above: *"Photographing a nest in a tree"*.

such a thing as jealousy did not enter into his composition, and he always took pains to give anyone the fullest credit due to him".[21]

Richard maintained a field diary throughout his life, the notes he made while waiting in hides often being transcribed more or less directly into his publications. The diaries have much to say about the working practices pioneered by the Kearton partnership, being eloquent of the occasional successes and numerous frustrations, disappointments and bad luck attending naturalist and photographer. Entry after entry records days that were rained off, birds that

Above: *"Ringed plover's eggs as laid; starling's eggs in the same nesting place".*

refused to sit, film that was spoiled, nests that were robbed. At times he was reduced to the most minor observations (e.g. "Saw and heard a magpie"). Typical is this: "Went into hide up for Peewit at 9.55 am and bird did not come back until 1.45 pm... Altogether spent 7 hours waiting for one snapshot and this turned out an abject failure on account of a piece of yew used as camouflage having blown over lens".[22]

In contrast, when conditions turned favourable, the naturalist photographer's mind had to work overtime: "June 26 1901. 7 time exposure of Thrush side on 8 spoilt. 9 rapid with stop. 8–10 absolutely open rapid shutter birds head in bad position. Missel Thrush I am studying sometimes brings half a dozen grubs at a time and divides them equally amongst her chicks. Occasionally she brings a bit of grass with them by accident and on rare occasions swallows the last grub she has in her bill herself. 11 spoilt, 12 spoilt, 17 bird sitting, 18 on edge of nest, 4 ditto quick exposure... The chicks were constantly preening themselves, stretching, flapping their tiny wings and bustling about the nest. On an average young were fed 4 times an hour but sometimes neither parent turned up for over an hour..."

Time spent waiting for photographic opportunities could yield

useful observations, as evinced in this diary entry from 29 May 1899: "Montagu's Harrier 8½ outside diameter. Nest made of rushes, sedges, ragwort stems and some dead grass. A big nest for 2 eggs. Nesting materials added as bird lays eggs. Marsh Harriers always lay their nests on the reeds etc., Montagu's always on the ground in a little cleared or pressed-down plain. Montagu's always press everything down near the nest".

In part, his field studies were for pragmatic reasons: the earning he made demanding new material for new lectures, he went out because he "required a film of a toad" for his next programme. But there is something insatiable in Richard's lust for nature knowledge, as demonstrated in his analysis of an abandoned longtailed tit's nest, which he picked up and "counted feathers in it, 300 and a little over belonging to—Wood pigeon, Pheasant, Songthrush, Blackbird, Rook, Robin and Chaffinch".[23] In this, his curiosity is akin less, perhaps, to forensic zoology, and closer to that informing archival and analytic trends in contemporary art, such as Herman de Vries's $1m^2$, the record in book form of an intervention in which every plant in a square metre of meadow was separated, identified and photocopied.

Any small discovery or observation could provide the trigger for

Kearton to make a further local wildlife experiment of a quasi-scientific nature, for its own sake:

> "Dec 6 1902. Whilst seeking a feeding stump, I turned over one with a live bluebottle under it. Brought him home in a matchbox and put him out of window along with a beetle (ascertain species) in another box and a thermometer. Freezing hard and at 6 o'clock thermometer down to 22°—yet bluebottle able to run about and buzz. Beetle absolutely still and lifeless. Beetle began to move one leg slightly at 40°—reared himself up on his legs table-like at 48°. Began to sleepily groom himself at 50° and to pull his jaws open at 54°. Basked in warm, leaning over sideways to do it from 56° to 60° and commenced to walk about at 67°."

Having photographed daisies asleep and awake for *Wild Nature's Ways*, he returned to probe the subject further in 1904. The speed of opening of daisies under a bucket was compared with those in the sun, the results being as one might suppose. After this the trials became more intense:

> "1. Dandelion did not close altho' placed in absolute darkness, neither did daisies until other flowers outside closed. 2. Daisies partly opened in dark when others did so outside, but dandelions did not. Daisies did not close again at same time as others did outside. Daisies in dark box did not open but as soon as they were in sun (3 pm) they opened out in ten minutes. Dandelion did not open a bit in 10 minutes sunshine. Dandelions showed no sign of opening after 15 minutes sunshine. Daisies on window sill remained quite open when others in fields were closed at 4.45 pm. Weather dull. 7 pm. Daisies not closed yet. 10.15 pm. Daisies closed."[24]

Local flora suffered further indignities when the Keartons came to photographing butterflies and other winged insects feeding. All too often the subject would move out of focus at the crucial moment, flying up and resettling on the "wrong" flower. Richard's solution was, on finding a place one frequented, to "remove every flower but one within a given area, then cutting a model butterfly out of a piece of newspaper, sticking it on the flower and obtaining a good clear focus…"[25] before the hapless creature returned. They found that smearing honey on flowers was an effective way of attracting red admirals in the autumn, while "during summer months great

Right: *Small tortoiseshell butterfly.*

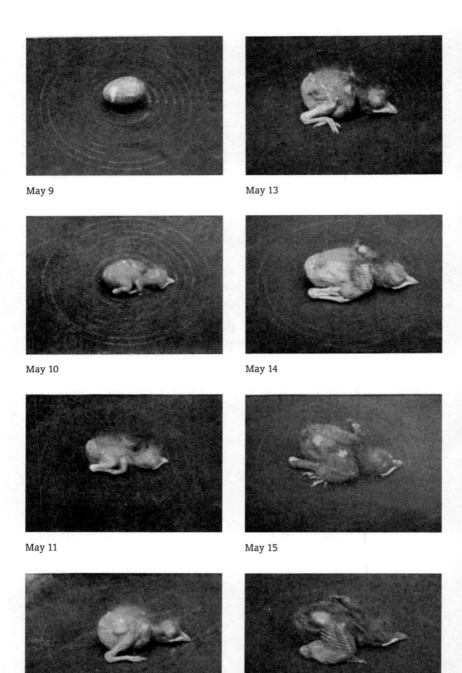

May 9

May 10

May 11

May 12

May 13

May 14

May 15

May 16

sport may be enjoyed, and good pictures obtained by 'sugaring' for moths".[26] This consisted of painting tree-trunks about four feet from the ground with "a mixture of treacle, rum and jargonelle pears"; best results were obtained on "a warm, cloudy evening, with the wind in the south or west". On some evenings, thirty or forty trees could be sugared without attracting a single moth, but when conditions were favourable, the Keartons would walk from tree to tree with bulls-eye lantern, camera and flash-lamp, and photograph their pick of whatever sugar-drowsy moths and beetles they found.

Photographic comparative pairs and series were used by the Keartons to demonstrate organic change, in much the way that the stills sequences of Edweard Muybridge had shown movement. One example contrasted, as we have seen, the appearance of daisies, asleep and awake; others included a hedgehog, rolled up and unrolled; and the tracks in snow of a bird walking, compared to one hopping. Breast feathers of a heron were compared with those of a gannet; tail quills of greater-spotted woodpecker with corncrake; flight feathers of swift with partridge. One of a pair of photographs showed the batch of four eggs of a ringed plover, where they had been laid on a stony foreshore; in the other, they were replaced with four starling eggs (see pp.70–71), as an object-lesson to "bring home to one the value of harmonising colours when there is no nest in a rather striking manner".[27]

One of the most informative of the photographic series was taken daily over the period 9–16 May 1900, showing the first week in the life of a baby blackbird.[28] Accuracy was ensured by fixing the camera on wooden pegs driven into the ground; at ten o'clock each morning, the chick was removed from its nest and placed at the bullseye of a target of concentric chalk rings drawn on a black board, where it was photographed. The series began with the intact egg on the last day before the chick hatched; for the first three days it lay quite still; on the fourth began to struggle, and "on the following day his eyes were partly open". On the seventh day, when the bird's feathers were starting to shoot, he "grew very uneasy... and began to kick, struggle and roll about", while the following day "he made very free use both of his legs and his wings", and "said some very nasty things about natural history photographers". To Richard's great grief, the series came to an unnatural—or perhaps only too natural—conclusion when the chick and its siblings were slain by a cat on the final day.

The idiosyncrasy of the techniques Richard sometimes employed

Left: *"The first week in a baby blackbird's life"*.

Above: *"Young nightjars in, and separated from, their natural surroundings"*.

was highlighted when he "made an experiment" upon a great mullein in a local meadow.[29] Behind the plant he placed a backboard ruled with a one-inch grid of lines, with his watch attached to the top of the board. He used a stick and length of string to support the stem of the mullein, which he then, by means unknown, "seriously injured". A sequence of five photographs taken at fifteen-minute intervals showed the "astonishing results" of the attack: the stem not miraculously recovering—which really would have astonished us—but, rather more predictably, gradually drooping into collapse.

*

> "Take my advice, boys and girls: don your strongest boots and go out to hear the birds sing their first morning hymn—it is the freshest and gladdest of all the day".[30]

Richard declared himself puzzled that he had upon his shoulders what he believed to be "the most unmusical head to be found in a whole country",[31] yet never had any difficulty in distinguishing the call notes and songs of birds, whereas various of his musical

acquaintances were at a loss to tell one bird sound from another. He advised that "the best time to hear Nature's choir is about four o'clock on a fine still morning during the first week in June, when the air is cool and sweet and every blade of grass bears its twinkling diamond of dew".[32] Some of his descriptions of bird vocalizations are among his most persuasive writing:

> "A starling's own song is a chissicking, creaking, snapping, rusty sort of production, with a few finer notes that are mostly borrowed dropping out here and there at intervals as if by accident, and the wing-flapping, throat-vibrating fuss it makes over its vocal efforts is really ludicrous".[33]

Robert Browning, in some of the most familiar lines in bird poetry,[34] suggested why the song thrush "sings each song twice over"; Richard Kearton found a metaphor that appears to define the song in its entire complexity, when he wrote that it "always reminds me of the methods of a clever preacher with a good voice. The loud, clear notes repeated in order to hammer home some important truth, the exquisite pauses in order to let them sink in, the low, sweet pleading and the cheerful ring of hope, are all there".[35]

Richard's published notes outlined the distinctions between song and sub-song, calls and alarms, innate song and taught song. An observation of a less familiar aspect of bird vocalization, made when visiting St Kilda, concerned the role in a flock of gannets of a sentinel bird[36] that would "keep watch at night while the other members of the species slumber". He learned that if local inhabitants were heard trying to catch gannets at night, the sentinel would cry out *"Beero!"* which he interpreted as meaning "Beware". On hearing this, the fowlers would stay silent and quite still; if satisfied, the sentinel may then sound the all-clear with *"Gorrok! gorrok!"*; if not, the repeated alarm would call the colony to instant flight.

A significant part of Richard Kearton's output was the books he wrote for children. Most of these appeared in the years 1900–1912, their origins probably lying in the education and entertainment of his own children. Three are story books, "stories told by mother birds to amuse their chicks and overheard by Richard Kearton, F.Z.S." as the sub-title of the first, *Strange Adventures in Dicky Bird Land* (1901), has it. Although such anthropomorphism might suggest that these are examples of the "nature faking" that both Keartons would later take a stand against, in fact the stories are based wholly on observation, and the behaviour of the protagonists is, excepting their ability to speak and express motives, characteristic and true to life. "I think I can claim one novel feature at least for the little volume. It is, so far as I know, the first work of fiction to be illustrated throughout from actual photographs of the characters living and moving within its pages."[37]

The other two story books, *The Adventures of Cock Robin and His Mate* (1904), and *The Adventures of Jack Rabbit* (1911), were won at the cost of considerable effort to obtain as many photos as possible of these individual species in the widest variety of poses and groupings. As books intended to instil young readers with a love of nature they work; what constrained them was that the only parts of the action that could be illustrated were those for which suitable photographs could be obtained. There is also a slightly awkward cognitive disjuncture between the realism of the photographs and the pretence of the conversations, something carried off to much greater effect in the alliance of text with the painted and drawn illustrations of, for example, Beatrix Potter or E. H. Shepard. A later book, *Wild Bird Adventures* (1923), of stories for a slightly older audience, advantageously separated the plates from the text pages, and was unusual in identifying the locations, mostly in Cumbria and Surrey, where the stories are set. (Previous volumes followed the policy adopted in *Our Rarer British*

Above: *"Squirrel at breakfast"*.

Breeding Birds, that illustrations and text "avoid as far as possible all chances of identification" to deter nest robbers).

The first of a number of reference and educational titles for children and young adults was *Our Bird Friends: A Book for All Boys and Girls* (1900), described by its author as a "chatty, though, so far as care and pains can make it, accurate little volume" whose chapters detail feeding, nests and eggs, offspring, flight and song. *The Fairyland of Living Things* (1907) covers the broader canvas of all the wild animals likely to be encountered in the British Isles, a sparky and imaginative collation of information, observation and anecdote within a small volume. The third title in this category, *Baby Birds at Home* (1912) describes and illustrates in all sixty-four species, a happy use of the Keartons' resource of numerous photographs of chicks on the nest or newly emerged.

In 1900 Cherry, with his hunger for the next new thing, acquired an Edison Bell wax-cylinder recorder and repeater, the first sound recording device to appear on the market. It came with a price tag of £50. It seems extraordinary to us now, but although birdsong had already been captured on such a machine—notably the claim by Ludwig Koch that in 1889, at the age of eight, he had recorded a captive Indian shama at Frankfurt Zoo—at this date the sound of a bird singing in the wild had never been recorded. There appeared to be a huge potential here, for creating the first library of bird sounds, just as the Keartons had set out to do eight years earlier with a catalogue of photographs of birds' nests and eggs.

Sadly, Cherry Kearton never had the opportunity to attempt widespread recording, as he was unable to overcome the technical problems associated with recording non-captive subjects. A flaw inherent in the Edison design was that the one machine acted as both recorder and player, the horn receiver doubling as loudspeaker. This resulted in a seemingly insoluble operating Catch–22: as soon as the bird began to sing, and the machine was put into action, the noise of the stylus cutting the wax was amplified through the horn, disturbing the bird and curtailing the song. In fact, it would be another three decades before better equipment, including remote microphones, would enable the reality of quality field recording of wildlife sounds (with Koch again in the vanguard). But Cherry took his Edison machine to the woodland garden of a house in Firs Road, Kenley, Surrey,[38] in the early mornings of the mating season of April and May 1900. It was a cold spring, cold enough to crack the wax cylinders. After numerous thwarted attempts, Cherry succeeded in capturing a perfunctory few bars of a nightingale and song thrush. Despite this earning him the accolade of first person in the world to record a bird singing in the wild, he pragmatically recognised that this particular pursuit was, for now, a blind alley, and the Edison was abandoned.

The other technological advance of the years of the Kearton partnership was their venture into film making, which began with

Right: *"Where I made the phonograph record of the nightingale singing in 1900"*.

Above: *"Tree pipit feeding a young cuckoo"*.

Cherry's acquisition of a cine camera around 1903; as with still photography, he mastered the basics himself before teaching Richard. The brief sequences, of a few feet of film shot here and there, were spliced together thematically to make shorts, typically of five minutes or so duration. Close-ups of individual birds in flight were obviously beyond the scope of early hand-cranked cine cameras, so the action shots are mostly of birds on the ground, nesting or swimming, or flying in flocks above colonies: the broad sweep of the breeding grounds could be shot from a much greater distance than the single subject. Details of the Keartons' early films are sketchy, made more so by the common practice of making new titles by resplicing old footage into fresh sequences. Records show that at least six distinct Kearton shorts, distributed by the Urban Trading Company, were shown at the Alhambra Theatre in 1907 and 1908.

A flavour of the novelty of "moving pictures" is given in the minutes of a meeting of the British Ornithologists' Club at Pagani's Restaurant, Great Portland Street, on 9 April 1908,[39] when "Mr. Cherry Kearton exhibited a wonderfully fine series of cinematograph pictures of bird-life" before "a very enthusiastic audience", which included fellow nature photographers R. B. Lodge and William Farren.

The first film screened, *Sea Bird Colonies*, showed gannets, cormorants, guillemots, puffins and terns on the Farne Islands and Bass Rock, "not only when at rest, but when swimming and flying, with a vividness that was truly astonishing". *Wild Birds at Home* illustrated a variety of birds feeding and brooding their chicks, and cleaning their nests, the audience being particularly taken with the sparrow hawk feeding its downy young: "The way in which the parent bird tore up the prey, and distributed a share to each nestling, was most beautifully shown, and was a perfect lesson in natural history". The writer noted that "so excellent and realistic did the pictures seem, that the spectators could scarcely believe they were not actually watching the living birds themselves". Cherry was rewarded with loud applause and the warmest thanks and hearty congratulations of the chairman for "the wonderful pictures just shown, the results of so much skill and indomitable patience".

Cinematography offered the ideal medium for a continuation of the forensic studies of nature—those particular branches of nature one might encounter on an English country walk—initiated by Richard Kearton with the photographic pairs and series of daisies, dandelions, fledgling birds and so on, in themselves the shortest of proto-films with the smallest number of frames. But he never explored the possibilities of moving film as innovatively as he had still photography; whether this was due to his ambivalence toward the value of cinema is not clear, but his films remained principally substantive. We have to look elsewhere to find reflections of that early Kearton brilliance, to the film work especially of two contemporary pioneers. F. Percy Smith loved to feed his audience "the powder of instruction in the jam of entertainment", from his early masterpiece *Birth of a Flower*, through insect close-ups achieved using "original (and bizarre) methods for time lapse and micro cinematography"[40] to the *Secrets of Nature* series he made for British Instructional Films. And walking very much in the Keartons' footsteps, O. G. Pike, who had already developed the 'Birdland' stills camera, made influential early films such as *In Birdland* (1907) and *St Kilda: Its People and Birds* (1908), leading to the groundbreaking cinematic detective work of *The Cuckoo's Secret* of 1922. As following chapters relate, Cherry Kearton went on to take up film in a bigger way; and with bigger creatures, on larger continents.

CHAPTER FOUR

The stuffed ox and other hides

"To excel in deception is not a very laudable accomplishment, but the heinousness of the crime may, perhaps, be softened in the eyes of the moralist by a knowledge of the fact that in this case the duplicity employed has been as entirely harmless to the deceived as it has been profitable to the deceiver.

Nature's children do not reveal their intimate ways to the bustling, human noise-maker, and he who would seek to know something of their interesting daily doings must first of all acquire the faculty to observe whilst remaining unobserved, and hear without being heard."

—Richard Kearton, *Wild Nature's Ways*, p.1.

Once the nests and eggs of most British breeding birds had been catalogued on film, the next challenge would surely be a photographic encyclopedia of the birds themselves. In the event, it would take another three decades before this was attempted; Richard, by then in poor health and in the last years of his life, published the *Pocket Book of British Birds* in 1925, a joint venture with his son-in-law, Howard Bentham, the text of the work being "the result of his knowledge, methodical care and industry". The format predicted the Observer's Book series of field guides, which would be launched with a volume devoted to *British Birds* in 1937. The *Pocket Book*, whose descriptions of a total of 265 species were "at once simple, terse, up-to-date and reliable", was "believed to contain the most complete collection of photographs of British birds ever brought within the covers of a small volume".[1]

This should have been among the Keartons' most notable trophies, and a fitting finale to Richard's career; in practice the small, black-and-white illustrations proved much less useful for identification than the colour drawings of rival publications, and the success of the book was modest. Despite Cherry Kearton's assertion that by the time of his first African trip in 1909 he had "photographed nearly every

Left: *"Wryneck at nesting hole"*.

bird found in the British Isles",[2] sixty-seven of the species described are not illustrated, including such relatively common types as siskin, knot and sanderling; others are represented by photographs of their nests and eggs; some photos, such as red-legged partridge and wood-cock—that at full-page size would have been instructive in showing the homogeneity of plumage and habitat—are useless at this scale; while in one or two cases, such as the mallard, it is hard to make out the bird at all.

We can begin to see why the project, an idea which Richard had "repeatedly turned in my mind", took so long when we look at the bird books following *British Birds' Nests*: what is striking is how few bird photographs they contain. Less than one third of the ninety-six illustrations in *Wild Life at Home*, for example, depict birds. About one half of these are opportune 'extras' from the birds' nests quest, show-ing more-or-less stationary adults on the nest, or chicks close to it; eight depict flocks, mostly seabirds, taken from a distance; and three are small vignettes used decoratively. In *With Nature and a Camera*, just two plates stand out as exceptional bird studies: one of a barn owl taken by flashlight, the other a kingfisher taken from behind one of the first hides, a wooden door.

The impasse was caused by the significant problem that had been dogging the Keartons: how to capture naturalistic studies of such shy, nervy creatures as birds. "The behaviour of nearly all wild crea-tures is one thing when they know they are being watched, and quite another when they are not aware of the fact. Under the first condi-tion, suspicion and anxiety are written large in every action, whereas under the second, confidence and peace of mind illuminate each movement and expression".[3] To obtain natural studies, they believed, it was essential not only to avoid disturbing the bird, but to be close enough to read its posture—its body language—without being seen. Hence the conundrum: how to position the unwieldy tripod and plate camera, and its alarming human operator, within a few feet of the subject, while remaining invisible. It was impossible, of course; but what might be possible was the use of camouflage to transform photographer into scenery.

One of their first attempts was the commission, perhaps from their sister-in-law Frances who was a dressmaker, of matching suits and caps of reversible material, dead grass-brown on one side and living meadow-green on the other, made "to observe and remain unob-served in, under differing conditions of colour surroundings".[4] These

Right: *"Artificial tree-trunk open"*.

outfits came with wooden masks fashioned from hollow ash-stubs, selected and cut by an old woodman, lightened by chiselling out much of the interior, and finished with comedy-sleuth eyeholes. When Richard was watching a family of bullfinches bathing at an old tub, one bird alighted on the mask, and "the telephonic qualities of the wood made the noise produced by its feet sound as if a rook had settled there".[5] The masks worked well enough, but only of course for visual surveillance. Something more elaborate would be needed to hide both photographer and camera.

They experimented in 1898 with an artificial tree trunk,[6] a stage-prop like contraption built around a slender wigwam of three 7-foot bamboo struts, contoured with wooden hoops, galvanised mesh and fabric, which Richard's wife Ellen camouflaged with paint (including trompe l'oeil bird droppings), and Cherry adorned with pieces of moss and lichen. There was just sufficient space inside for the photographer standing hard against his camera, whose tripod legs could be only partially spread. The results were promising—a fine study of a wryneck on a tree trunk was obtained—but the hide would only do for tree- or hedge-nesting subjects, in situations where the fake tree would blend in and where there was sufficient light for the necessarily short exposure. Having explored its potential, and realised its limits, the Keartons set their minds to something with a more versatile application for the ground-feeding and nesting birds of pastureland.

In the winter of 1899, Richard Kearton paid a visit to his "old friend" Rowland Ward, at 166 & 167 Piccadilly, London. Ward was—figuratively only, as far as we know—the taxidermist's taxidermist, whose declared ambition was "to begin at that point in taxidermy where the old school left off... to study nature and adapt it, in connection with modelling, to the taxidermist's art". The old school, of course, was familiar from the country piles of Norfolk and the Scottish Highlands, with their ubiquitous mounted stags' heads and stuffed birds of prey. But it was the fashion for hunting in India and Africa that had inspired Ward's new direction. Here, in the showrooms he had named 'The Jungle', one could stumble upon elephant-foot waste-paper baskets, crocodile umbrella stands, tiger-skull lamps, rhino-foot doorstops, tortoise musical boxes and—one of the most popular lines—the rampant black bear dumb waiter. Tiger, leopard and zebra hides lent their exotic patterns to rugs and upholstered chairs; a whole range of household knick-knacks could be had

Left: *"Artificial tree-trunk closed"*.

from the hooves of ungulates, including match boxes, tobacco jars, ink pots, book-ends and bells.[7]

Kearton was at Piccadilly to tell Rowland Ward to expect an animal hide he would despatch for mounting, according to special instructions. Not only would the finished article have to be as realistic as possible, but also strong enough to mount, and light enough to carry on the shoulder. The hide was an unusual subject for Ward, having come from neither the glens of the north nor the jungles of the east, but from its native habitat of the Surrey pastures. And it had been acquired not in the hunt, but from a butcher. The animal was an ox, and Kearton wanted it mounted standing up.

The commission accepted, Ward had the hide sent first to one of the commercial tanneries, possibly J. Whitehead of Hommerton, to be cured, tanned and dried, a process requiring several weeks. It was then forwarded to Ward's workshops at Leighton Place in Kentish Town for mounting. Ordinarily the framework would have consisted of a vertical centre board—the top edge replicating the contours of the spine—from which were extended legs of iron rod whose feet were anchored to a wooden base. But the need for additional rigidity, and for the allowance of as much space as possible in the interior, suggested to Ward the adaptation of his technique for the preservation of larger specimens, such as rhino and elephant. In lieu of the centre board a hollow wooden carapace, like an inverted hull, would substitute the backbone and ribs. And since the ox was to be used for the purposes of deception the wooden baseboard was ruled out, in turn precluding the iron rods, which would have been too pliant unanchored. Instead, the legs were formed in deal, with two rods supporting the skull—by now boiled clean—and a length of heavy wire to hold the tail. (The tail was, in fact, completely stiff, aligned down the hindquarters even when the ox was inverted. One can't help feeling the Keartons missed a trick in not borrowing from stagecraft a mechanical pulley to enable the final touch of verisimilitude, a swishing tail.)

The framework of the carcass was fleshed out with 'excelsior', the wood wool then commonly used for packing, attached in a thick layer with twine: a skilled job if the most realistic contours were to be obtained. Which was evidently the case; so well was it stuffed that "during its palmy days before it had been blown over and otherwise injured, it was several times mistaken, when out in the fields, for a live animal".[8] Finally, the hide was stitched into place. The whole job would have taken one man about a week.

On Sunday, 20 May 1900, the finished item was dispatched in a cart to Ardingley, Richard Kearton's residence in Caterham Valley,

Above: *"The stuffed ox in operation"*.

where it must have seemed a wonderful toy to his daughters Dora, then aged 10, and Grace, 8, although "a young son of one of our neighbours was badly scared by it when he saw a seemingly real live ox staring over the hedge".[9] The following Wednesday the Keartons put the stuffed ox into action. Up the chalk track past Tillingdown Farm, dropping into the rough scoop of Great Dene valley and over the old rifle range, clambering the far incline toward Birchwood, and so to a long, plateau-like meadow. This was part of the Marden Park estate, once home to William Wilberforce, now owned by Mr (later Sir) Walpole Greenwell, who had granted the Keartons permission to carry out their work on his land. A breeder of shorthorn cattle, Greenwell might have taken a closer than usual interest in this particular venture.

The Marden Park meadow was part of Richard's Kearton's regular stamping ground, and he knew that here was a promising first subject, a skylark's nest with young. The ox was set up within five feet of the nest; and then, as Kearton described it: "Admission to the interior is gained through a long horizontal slit in the skin of the underparts, and the camera, minus the legs of the tripod, fixed upon a little platform in the brisket. The lens peeps out of a hole in the skin of the breast, and through another and smaller aperture above

Above: *"Artificial rubbish-heap"*.

it the photographer watches his field of focus". Hunched over his camera, Kearton didn't have long to wait. The lark returned to the nest, apparently completely deceived by the bullock, for "she came again and again, without hesitation, to feed her chicks". The Keartons delightedly recorded "the pleasant satisfaction of having a long-cherished idea so completely justified, and the exhilarating rapidity with which pictures of the lark were added".[10]

There was a danger that their belief in the totality of the deception might have triggered the old family bugbear, rashness. They couldn't have been certain that the stuffed ox was not tainted with the danger of human presence, and moving it abruptly so close to the nest risked alarming parents and jeopardising young. In fact, two years previously they had photographed another lark's nest with young using a different hide, the artificial rubbish heap. This was constructed out of an old umbrella whose ribs had been extended with bamboo, the whole covered with heavy linen on top of which natural materials were heaped. In Richard's account it was "thatched with wisps of straw", but Cherry, who as often as not was underneath, remembered "leaves and sticks and dirt", and how Richard would "pile all the rubbish he could find".[11] The artificial rubbish heap proved versatile and saw service over a number of years and in a variety of situations, including the Eden valley in June 1900, when it was used to photograph a peewit on the nest, redstart, sandpiper and wheatear. In deploying it, they took the sensible precaution of setting the hide up some distance from the nest and moving it gradually closer before putting it to use. They don't record why it was thought unnecessary to employ this stratagem with the ox, but presumably reasoned that the sudden arrival of a heap of straw was suggestive of human activity, whereas that of an ox was not.

Any confidence in this argument was undermined by the unforeseen effects of "the awful pain I began to suffer in my lumbar regions through stooping over the camera so long in the Jonah-like quarters afforded by the interior of the ox". Richard Kearton was at last compelled "by sheer agony" to drop from his place of concealment while the lark was at the nest. "Upon catching sight of me she sprang almost vertically into the air, and, dropping amongst the grass a yard or two behind her nest, stared with outstretched neck in blank amazement at me sprawling beneath the bullock".[12]

No harm was done on this occasion as the bird did not desert her nest. If anything, the incident highlighted the great care the Keartons usually took to avoid disturbing their subject. This was an aspect of the moral responsibility in their attitude to wildlife; in the opening sentence of *Wild Nature's Ways*, in which the brothers' exploits with the stuffed ox are related, Richard suggested with tongue in cheek that this extended even to their use of concealment: "To excel in deception is not a very laudable accomplishment, but the heinousness of the crime may, perhaps, be softened in the eyes of the moralist by a knowledge of the fact that in this case the duplicity employed has been as entirely harmless to the deceived as it has been profitable to the deceiver".[13]

The other motive for avoiding disturbance was, of course, to obtain the best photographs. The Keartons' experiments in this area were radical and instructive. Early trials showed that birds were disturbed by the "great eye" of the camera lens, the click of the shutter, and by human presence. The first concern was addressed by concealing the lens with camouflage, as far as possible; the second, by the use of the almost-silent window-blind shutter and, as Richard would discover while photographing a merlin from a heather hide (see below), sound trauma could be mitigated over time by releasing the shutter repeatedly until the bird became familiarised. As for the greater fear of humans, they discovered that if the bird saw the photographer enter his hide and not emerge, she would remain alarmed, whereas if an assistant were to accompany the photographer, "tuck him in" and ostentatiously walk away, the symptoms of alarm would desist.

For the present, the Keartons found the stuffed ox "an admirable hiding place", although it appeared to have had one fatal drawback: "if used during breezy weather, it is liable to be blown over", Richard wrote. "I remember once returning to see how my brother was faring whilst waiting for some subject, and arrived upon the scene just in time to witness man and beast occupying a very undignified position. The back of the ox had landed in a slight declivity, and the feet of both biped and quadruped were pointing towards the zenith..." In future, they took "four pegs and a quantity of string out with us. The former are driven firmly into the ground, and the bullock's legs lashed securely to them by means of the latter".[14]

Cherry later reported it was not the wind that had toppled the ox, rather that the disorienting effect of the murky interior, with the sole visual reference the small hole in the neck, had caused him to either faint or lose balance after only ten minutes, causing man and beast to capsize.[15] In his account of the incident, Richard had returned not "just in time", but an hour after ox and photographer had become inverted. And even then, characteristically, Richard had stopped to take a photograph of his brother's predicament before helping him recover his dignity. The drollery that the Keartons would play up to was sometimes farcical, as in the much-reproduced studies of Cherry inside the ox waving his legs in the air, or hoisting the beast inverted on his shoulder; more often there is a dry wit informing, for example, the choice of caption for a full-page plate of the dumb, stolid woodenly-posed ox, staring vacantly across a meadow: "The Stuffed Ox in Operation". By this time, the Keartons were used to playing to the house, and capitalized on the added value of setting up for the camera in poses that anticipated the deadpan slapstick of silent comedians such as Buster Keaton.

In the same meadow as the lark's nest was a man-made feature characteristic of this pervious downland: a dew pond, a clay-lined dug-out for watering cattle. The weather being "excessively hot at the time", this was much frequented by thirsty cattle and birds. The stuffed ox was added to the community, and "distinguished itself by completely deceiving every species of creature that came to drink". The Keartons were able to secure at this single location photographs of "pheasants, jays, ring doves, turtle doves, stock doves, song thrushes, blackbirds, yellowhammers, greenfinches, chaffinches and sparrows".[16] Incidentally, the little oasis of the pond would become a regular photography and bird-watching haunt for Richard, who took

Above: *"Mounted on the imitation ox".*

it upon himself to clear it of weeds and rubbish every June; on my last visit, it was thickly overgrown with hawthorn, elder and brambles.

One of the photographs taken at the pond gives a good idea of the capabilities and expectations of nature photography at that time. Richard Kearton was focussing on a jay which "without showing any signs of being ready to take his departure... suddenly sprang into the air and flew away". Kearton instantly released his shutter, but when the plate was developed "suffered the extreme mortification of finding that he had just managed to get his head out of the plate, and his portrait, with wings beautifully stretched out and legs still ungathered in, was guillotined". The appearance of such a photograph, with subject intact, in a wildlife magazine today would perversely seem to us not the "ornithological photograph of a lifetime", as it was gauged by Kearton, but almost commonplace and at entry level to merit publication. Kearton was being, as ever, pragmatic; he knew that he was testing the limits of the plate camera in static studies of flighty

Above: *"Stuffed sheep"*.

subjects, and under those conditions a quality study of a bird on the wing would depend on much good luck.[17]

The stuffed ox reveals, too, an insight into the work of the Keartons: if it enabled the complete disappearance of the photographer, both physically and as an influence on his subject—essential, if studies were to be made of the unaffected behaviour of wildlife—and worked as "a sort of extinguisher for the camera", it also militated for absolute objectivity, for the absence of the photographer's psychological investment, the baggage of his sentiment. Taking turns in the ox to photograph ring doves and turtle doves, the two Keartons were surprised to discover that "we had both photographed our birds in almost identical actions, attitudes and situations". The illustrations to the published works of the Keartons were advertised as being taken "direct from Nature", and one of their strengths lies in this disqualification of personal intervention.

A major contributor to the Keartons' lasting reputation, the stuffed ox had a brilliant but surprisingly brief working life, being deployed in May and July 1900 and retired at the end of the season. Its ultimate fate is unrecorded, although it would be nice to think that it might have had one final role, perhaps standing in for the effigy of that other undercover agent, Guy Fawkes, atop a bonfire.

A flurry of naturalistic and site-specific hides was tried out over the two seasons following the success of the ox, commencing with a second livestock hideaway, the stuffed sheep—not a Swaledale, but a Suffolk or Blackface—which unlike its predecessor was set up sitting down. It was commissioned from a local taxidermist, Charles Thorpe of Croydon, and on 21 May 1901 taken by Richard in the guard's van of a train to Kirkby Stephen, where he was staying with his uncle Cherry. This is one of the earliest photographic trips we know of when Richard was unaccompanied by brother Cherry, and he worked alone, or with the help of his uncle or locally recruited volunteers.

The sheep, intended to blend in on the moorland of Cumbria, was used with some success in the first week of June 1901, for the photography of wheatears, meadow pipits and sandpipers in the Potts Valley area. The size limitation meant that the camera had to be operated remotely. It was positioned, minus the legs of the tripod, on a firm stone in front of the nest, focussed and loaded with a plate; a fifty-foot length of pneumatic tubing was attached to the shutter release, and extended to a vantage point overlooking the nest. The carapace of the sheep was then placed over the camera, and the chest wool tied back so that it would not wave in front of the lens. Kearton then set up his hiding tent, covered it with rushes, and took his place inside. The greater distance introduced a haphazard element into the satisfactory timing of shots, and the first deployment—on a pair of sandpipers—suggested the sheep would be suitable only for subjects sitting on the nest.

But while waiting for the sandpipers, Richard noticed a pair of wheatears feeding their young, which nearly every time they came along with food "alighted for a moment on a view-commanding stone close by their nesting hole". Richard hoisted the sheep onto his back, moved the rest of his gear into place and focussed on "a match-box placed on the top of the stone to represent the body of a bird". Knowing he was dealing with a bolder species, he was able to erect the hiding tent much closer than before. A telling shot of the male wheatear passing over food to the female to take to the young was the reward (see p.99). But such were the limitations of the stuffed sheep that its career was doomed to be no lengthier than that of the Ox, and it seems likely that when he took the return journey south, Richard travelled alone.[18]

That same week, when up on Nateby Fell he heard a merlin call, and located its nest in the heather. He marked the spot with a pile of foliage and returned the next day to photograph. The location suggested a variation on the rubbish heap: this was his hiding tent "which consists of eight iron legs a quarter of an inch in diameter, six feet in length, eyeleted at the top to a small ring, and covered with a skirt-shaped light canvas", set up within twelve feet of the nest, and thatched all over with heather. Kearton retired to a distance to see how the birds would react, and had the satisfaction of seeing the merlin alighting on the structure before returning to the nest. In the afternoon, Richard had his friend Willie Alderson tuck him into the heather house and walk away. The merlin went to ground and "I suppose catching sight of lens flopped about in heather all round for about 20 minutes, then she went on to nest". Having grown accustomed to the lens, the bird was next alarmed by the sound of the shutter: the first time or two it was operated "she went off her eggs in a great hurry", but by the end of two hours she became so used to the noise "that she sat like a brick and when I had exposed all my plates I could not get rid of her by tapping focusing glass or legs of camera so threw my water bottle out from back of hide up".[19]

When he made his annual visit to the Fells in May and June the following year, Richard took with him another prefabricated hide-away. This was a lightweight artificial rock, again commissioned from Charles Thorpe; we know that it was in "five easily adjustable pieces", a flat-pack of four walls and a roof, large enough to accommodate photographer and camera, and painted limestone-grey; the exact mode of construction is not apparent, but it was most probably stretched canvas or thin ply on deal frames. Richard fixed it up near a dipper's nest in Potts Valley, "a wonderful little ghyll for bird life", where he had recorded thirty-eight species. The rock was left overnight mounted on top of an existing large boulder, and moved in the morning behind a crag close to the nest. The dippers took no alarm and Kearton was able to secure some good shots "despite the extreme difficulty of making even rapid exposures upon these eternally curtseying creatures", from a large number of fast plates. Even greater success was had when the artificial rock was set up before a curlew's nest in a "limestone boulder-strewn pasture not far distant". The rock was placed on the first day sixty yards from the nest, and moved a little closer, morning by morning, for a week, until within sixteen feet of nest and eggs. So completely was this "characteristically cunning bird" deceived, that after a while Kearton found photographing her on the nest became a thing of "monotonous ease", so that he took to mewing like a cat to provoke the bird into different postures and behaviour: walking away, glancing over

Right: *"Wheatears: male passing over food to female to take to young"*.

her shoulder, picking up and dropping straws, and thrusting her bill down the earth-shafts of dung beetles.[20]

A few days later, Richard was alerted by a shepherd to a nest with a brace of newly-hatched chicks of the golden plover on the moorland between Shunnerfell and Water Crag. The landscape here being open and featureless, with no natural cover, Kearton asked the shepherd to secure a spade and dig turves, from which between them the two men built a structure with horseshoe-shaped walls, as close as five feet from the nest. The sod house was completed with a roof supported by "the dilapidated remains of a neighbouring sheep-fold gate". The plovers proved nervous sitters, made so restless by the sound of the shutter that Kearton could secure only three plates of the parent birds, having knelt for two and a half hours "with water dripping steadily down the back of my neck from the roof sods of the emergency hide-up". But the chicks were soon strong enough to leave the nest, when a good fourth shot of one of them was obtained.[21]

Further opportunities to experiment with photographic hides came the following month when Richard travelled in the Outer Hebrides. Here he was determined to photograph oyster-catchers at nest. His hiding tent being unusable on the rocky shore, "the next best thing that suggested itself to my mind was a rough stone house". (This was something he had previously tried in May 1901, on a day when the wind was too strong to use the stuffed sheep for photographing meadow pipits by the beck in Potts Valley; the rudimentary stone shelter he resorted to building was abandoned when the wind blew so hard that "it knocked over part of my stone hide up and I narrowly escaped having some of my fingers broken"). The optimum site selected, Richard found that, inevitably, few of the stones near at hand were suitable, and "I was therefore compelled to carry a goodly number... a great distance on my back". From these he built walls that were, again, horseshoe-shaped, with an aperture facing the nest and doorway on the far side; a cache of driftwood was hauled from the crater where it had washed up, and used to complete the roof and partly bar up the doorway. The camera was focused by him placing his cap over the eggs, to represent the body of the bird. A local cowherd boy who was employed to tuck him in and walk away brought with him "the largest and heaviest cloth overcoat I ever beheld", sent for Richard's comfort by a "thoughtful Highland soul". Photographically, the stone house proved a success, but at the end of "three hours of cramped misery", with a "bitter wind whistling

Left: *"Male golden plover covering chick"*.

through every chink in the dry walls", Richard could take no more but "crawled forth and went my way, leaving the birds in peace". Nothing daunted, when he later found a ringed plover's nest a little way off, Richard built a second stone house of fresh material, sharing only the doorway timber of "Oyster-Catcher House" with "Ringed Plover Villa".[22]

The last of the secret houses was built to photograph the Arctic skua with nest, eggs and young on heather uplands in the Hebrides. Richard tried at first his hiding tent, but became convinced that the vibration of the canvas in the face of a strong wind was disturbing the birds. When he put a plan for "the erection of a turf hovel" to the local gamekeeper who had found the nest, he "immediately went off in search of a spade". They dug out a pit, almost hip deep, for the accommodation of Kearton's feet and legs, made a frame of the tent irons above it, and covered the whole in "great strips of turf". The day's work done, they left and had the satisfaction of seeing the skua return immediately to its nest. The following day the weather closed in, but despite the darkness, the waving of bent grass and heather, and the constant head movements of the bird, of the ten "more or less haphazard" exposures Richard made, a couple turned out "good beyond all expectation".[23]

In fact, the mimetic hides and autochthonous 'houses' enabled some of the Keartons' best bird photography, and as late as 1938 Cherry maintained "I do not think that they have ever been improved upon".[24] The costs, of course, were the considerable effort of their construction; the limitations of their site-specificity; in the case of the mimetic hides, their cumbrousness; and of the houses, their immobility. In the right situation, they continued to provide the best solution: later variations employed by the Keartons included, for example, a duck-hunting punt covered in reeds for photographing wildfowl on the Norfolk broads, and as late as 1908 a hastily-assembled hide of thorn sprays for a fox. Contemporary photographers continue on occasion to resort to improvised hides of native vegetation. The mimetic camera hide, too, still crops up from time to time, in the form of artificial rocks, blocks of ice and even elephant dung; sophisticated recent examples include the radio-controlled motorised robotic sea animals with cameras in their eyes, including a 'spy dolphin', 'spy tuna', 'spy ray' and 'spy sea turtle', used to great success to film underwater creatures such as the spinner dolphin, for the 2013 BBC series *Dolphins: Spy in the Pod*.

The Keartons were not unique in their experiments, a number of photographers in America especially having tried various conceal-

Above: *"Stone house for photographing oyster-catcher"*.

ments: the Wallihans recorded building something resembling a grouse butt as early as 1894; Francis Herrick used a tent blind in 1901, and Frank Michler Chapman (perhaps inspired by the Keartons) road-tested an umbrella blind about the same time. But by 1903 or 1904, the Keartons' charmingly eccentric sequence of adventures in this field had been eclipsed; they had learned that the job of the mimetic hide could be done by a simple all-purpose tent. This rather mundane outcome was profitable in revealing a flaw in the understanding of the reaction mechanism of birds; a flaw that could very easily have been sprung by the simple means of deploying a hide in the 'wrong' environs. It was, simply, the assumption that unfamiliarity was the key alarm trigger, and therefore to avoid apprehension it was necessary to use only materials which the subject bird would register as 'safe'. As the Keartons would discover, birds have, in fact, no such reflex. What does arouse suspicion and alarm is sights and sounds that are abrupt or indicative of predation. So, as it turned out, what the Keartons had achieved by their disguises with sheep, oxen, heathers and rocks could be achieved as well by canvas: a visual

Above: *"Kingfisher: the bird only came three or four times a day... and while photographic light lasted* [Cherry] *kept constant watch, even having some of his meals brought to him, for fear of missing a chance. Six days spent more or less in patient waiting...".*

neutrality that absented both photographer and equipment from the real alarm triggers that would arouse the bird's suspicion. What wildlife photographers use today is little evolved from what the Keartons ended up with, though the brothers would no doubt have appreciated the greater convenience and comforts of lightweight and weather-resistant materials, the ubiquitous polyester fabric printed with generic camouflage patterning, not to mention nature reserves with their wooden chalet-style hides with hinged viewing shutters.

That might have been the end of the story as far as the Keartons' deployment of mimetic hides is concerned. But when Cherry Kearton first visited East Africa in 1909, he was once again confronted by the problem of bringing the camera within range of the subject—in this case, large mammals. Having made the "exciting discovery" on his journey out of Nairobi that the hundreds-strong herds of zebra, wildebeest, kongoni, gazelles and other species were not afraid of the train, he made the assumption that "I shan't even have to stalk them: I can just go and set up my camera in the open, without a hide, and take all the photographs I want!" But when he got down to work on foot, away from the effective 'hide' of the locomotive, he found that herds would "bound away in terror when I walked within two hundred yards of them".[25]

At this point, remembering the ingenious hides he and Richard had employed in England, he wondered about "altering them to suit the locality; thus, instead of a dummy sheep, I thought I might have a dummy zebra". Luckily, he shared his thoughts with some local hunters. There was a crucial difference, they pointed out, between using a dummy hide to enter the secrets of the bird world in an English field—where a benign, stationary creature might happily be ignored—and attempting the same deception on the hierarchical animal kingdom of the Africa savannah, where it would be at the very centre of attention. The outcome, they reckoned, could only go one of two ways: either a trigger-happy hunter would bag the stuffed zebra first, or nature would take its course and the creature's astonishing—and astonished—inner secret be made known to the world, by a predatory lion or cheetah.[26]

....

CHAPTER FIVE

The man who shot Roosevelt in Africa

On 27 March 1909, Cherry Kearton embarked from Southampton, bound for Mombasa. He travelled with his brother-in-law, William Coates, a Fellow of the Zoological Society who had already spent some time in Africa. The two men were the only fare-paying passengers on board a cargo ship, the SS *Bardistan*. Four days earlier, Theodore Roosevelt and his son Kermit had sailed from Manhattan on the SS *Hamburg*, a German liner bound for Naples, on the first leg of a voyage to British East Africa. Roosevelt was to undertake an almost year-long safari, and Kearton was "fired with the idea that I should go there at the same time as he did, meet him and perhaps even join him in the bush".[1]

Roosevelt had just completed his second term in office as President of the United States of America. Energetic, impulsive, a Republican intellectual radical, in 1900 he was elected vice-president, succeeding a few months later at the age of 42 to office as the youngest president in American history when William McKinley was assassinated. Teddy Roosevelt's combination of charisma, earthiness and pragmatism made him immensely popular, and he was returned for a second term in 1904 with a landslide victory. During his presidency, he negotiated some outstanding political feats: ending the coal strike of 1902 with favourable terms for the miners; securing Panamanian independence, enabling the construction of the Panama Canal; mediating the end of the Russian-Japanese war, for which he was awarded the Nobel Peace Prize. Regarded as a national hero, he has been credited with doing more than anyone to forge the dynamic image of modern America as a world force in science, culture and politics.

An insatiable reader and polymath, 'Bull Moose' himself wrote 51 books, including a number on nature and wildlife. He had learned taxidermy as a young boy, and at the age of 23 donated some of his handiwork of over six hundred stuffed birds to the Smithsonian. Roosevelt was an animal lover, but it was not always clear if he loved them more alive or dead; an avid hunter, he was co-founder of

Left: *Cherry Kearton with colobus monkey.*

the Boone and Crockett Club, promoting hunting as a gentlemanly sport whose aim was to kill, but not overkill. During his presidency he became a champion of conservation, which on his terms referred as much to the safeguarding of tracts of primal landscape for hunting grounds as to the protection of species. He created five national parks and four national game refuges; eighteen national monuments, including the Grand Canyon; over fifty bird sanctuaries, and more than 100 million acres of national forest.[2]

In the spring of 1908, Roosevelt—still only 50 years of age—was contemplating what to do at the end of his presidency, having declared against standing for a third term in that year's election. Time out of the spotlight would allow him to consider his future, including the possibility of standing again in 1912, and would help the incoming candidate, the ineffectual William Taft, emerge from his shadow. He invited a number of eminent naturalists to the White House, including taxidermist Carl Akeley and the British conservationist and seasoned African lion-hunter Frederick Selous, to sound them out on a formative plan: to travel to East Africa, and undertake a safari.

This was the next new thing since the wild west was won, an inspired, if somewhat inevitable, choice for Roosevelt. The concept of safari—*journey*—which owed its ancient origins to Arab mercantile treks into the African interior with slave porters to collect oil, horn and ivory, had been borrowed in the mid-19th century by white missionaries and explorers, some to become household names: David Livingstone; H. M. Stanley; Cecil Rhodes; and Richard Burton, who introduced the word safari into the English language. It evolved further in the twenty years or so since colonialized Africa had been carved up between Western nations, with vast plots of land in British East Africa—present day Kenya and Uganda—being sold for farming and housing, largely to the aristocracy. Safari now became the vehicle of engineers and administrators, while for the developers it attracted a new breed: the adventurer sportsman. Their function was at first to clear the hills and plateaux, the 'White Highlands' that were most highly prized for grazing and for tea and coffee plantations, with the mass slaughter of big game (not always carried out so sportingly: Lord Delamere was rumoured to manage his thousands of acres using a Gatling machine gun). By about 1900, the modern phase of safari was established when it was recognised that the economically unattractive savannahs and other grassland plains could be exploited for recreational shooting, and later for photography and animal observation. Settlers cashed in on shooting vacations, while

Above: *"Engaging porters at Lake Naivasha for lion spearing trip"*.

outfitters set up in Nairobi; in 1908, the most successful of these, Newland & Tarlton, established an office in Piccadilly, next door to taxidermist Rowland Ward, offering the complete safari 'package'. An elite pastime for the super-rich had arrived, selling itself on the promise of "freedom, luxury, power, danger and excitement".[3]

The initial attraction for Roosevelt was to satisfy his lust for adventure and hunting, and provide a coming of age rite of passage for his son Kermit; over the course of discussions the safari's purpose was elevated from sporting holiday to a mission to secure animal specimens for the Smithsonian Institution. It would take ten months of feasting, shooting and trekking through what were then British East Africa and the Belgian Congo, into Uganda and on to southern Sudan, before decommissioning at Khartoum. Funding came principally from the Smithsonian and donations from Andrew Carnegie; Roosevelt's own expenses would be covered by income from his bulletins, published monthly in *Scribner's Magazine* and later in book form as *African Game Trails*.

Among the naturalists invited to advise the president was Richard

Above: *"The safari crossing the Amboni river"*.

Kearton. He had written a favourable review of Theodore Roosevelt's 1907 publication, *Good Hunting*, on a hot topical issue, nature faking. This supported objections first raised by naturalist and writer John Burroughs in the *Atlantic Monthly* against the literary depictions of the Reverend William J. Long, Ernest Thompson Seton, Jack London and others of animals as compassionate creatures intelligent enough to learn and reason. Burroughs's position, and that of Roosevelt, was that wild animals function for the most part on hard-wired instinct and have little or no capacity for learning from experience. Roosevelt saw any suggestion to the contrary as fictional sentimentalising, undermining the image he had nurtured of a rugged and raw wild nature informing the robust and masculine superiority of his nation; he wrote of preserving the "physical hardihood... sense of limitless freedom, and... remoteness and wild charm and beauty of primitive nature".[4] His detractors claimed Roosevelt was merely attempting to defend his ambivalent position as both nature lover and voracious hunter. The term 'nature faker' would eventually be used less specifically to describe writers and film-makers who were simply over-sentimental or anthropomorphic, who distorted their descriptions of what they saw for literary effect. In one later definition: "The boundary between fact and fiction and between scientist and artist was crossed when the nature writer imparted more drama to nature than was found".[5]

The two men corresponded, leading to Kearton being invited to spend a week at the White House. On 10 March 1908, he embarked unaccompanied from Liverpool for Boston on the *Ivernia*, travelling down to Washington via New York, undertaking some lectures on the way, and arriving at the White House on 4 April. They went bird watching on the Potomac River, and for Richard, limping through the undergrowth in pursuit of a very energetic and impatient president, it was simply a wonderful and memorable trip. In conversation, Roosevelt suggested that "Africa would present a field for animal photography which could not be equalled anywhere in the world",[6] recalling in a later speech that he had discussed with Kearton his hopes for a future of photographic, rather than shooting, safaris. Akeley and Selous would travel to Africa with Roosevelt, and it is hard to avoid the conjecture that Roosevelt's tacit purpose in meeting Kearton was to size him up for the job of expedition photographer; and easy to understand why Kearton, with his routines tailored to the various demands of family, work and uncertain health, would have had to refuse had the offer been made.

In the event, there was a stampede among the major studios applying to send an embedded film crew: William Selig offered to train Kermit as a cameraman, while the Edison Manufacturing Company pledged the negatives of any such film to the Smithsonian, after the demands of commerce had been satisfied. All were turned down. The reason given was that film crew, kit and support would make the complement—which already, it was calculated, would need to be 250-strong—unwieldy. Privately, it was Roosevelt's determination to keep the expedition off the front pages that led him to appoint a single official still photographer, his son Kermit.

The core team of Americans—the two Roosevelts, zoologist Edmund Heller, naturalists J. Alden Loring and Edgar A. Mearns—landed at Mombasa on 21 April 1909. Even at this time, Roosevelt was having second thoughts about the blanket ban on press coverage, having come to an arrangement at Naples with the journalist Warrington Dawson to send home sanctioned dispatches to satisfy public curiosity. Dawson and three other reporters set up in Nairobi, from where they filed almost daily accounts of the latest kills and locations, and which local landowners had had the honour of entertaining the entourage. In the music halls back home, Roosevelt imitators shot lion imitators; songs were written, and sung in the follies.

But it was the cinema that was pulling in the crowds. New venues were being thrown up in towns across America and Europe, and studios were barely able to keep up with demand (it was reported that, with the population of the USA standing at 92 million, nickelodeons were selling 26 million tickets each week). And the Roosevelt jamboree was the story of the season: one of the earliest animated cartoon shorts was *Theodore Roosevelt's Arrival in Africa*. Meanwhile in Chicago, the Selig Polyscope Company hired an actor (who did not look much like Roosevelt, but whose luggage was stamped with the initials T. R.) and bought from a local zoo some game animals, which they located to a plot in the Edendale district of Los Angeles. In April 1909, a film of *Roosevelt in Africa*, later retitled *Hunting Big Game in Africa*, was shot on a set resembling a jungle built inside a large cage. For added veracity, an old zoo lion was cornered, shot dead, skinned, and the carcass spit roasted over a camp fire. Selig declared it the most realistic faking that ever was done. As soon as reports of the first shooting of a lion came in from Nairobi, early in May 1909, the film was released. Its lack of authenticity did not deter the public, who filled local cinemas nationwide. Selig earned enough to build a permanent safari set in Hollywood, populated with a menagerie of beasts, where a series of 'wildlife' films was produced, including the first Tarzan movie in 1918.

If news of the Selig production got back to Africa, it would no doubt have been received badly. Roosevelt may not have minded the box office receipts—he was notoriously careless of finances—but would have resented the false light shone on his expedition. Perhaps he even began to have second thoughts about having dismissed the idea of a real film record being made.

Kearton and Coates, meanwhile, had arrived at Mombasa around the beginning of May, and travelled on the Uganda Railway to the raw little town that was growing rapidly on safari money, Nairobi, where they checked in at the mock-Tudor Norfolk Hotel, with much to think about. "Though I had read a good many books on Africa I had... only a very vague idea of what I should find when I got there", Kearton admitted. He had been expecting "a jungle of tangled trees and vines and undergrowth, through which elephants and rhinos would come crashing mightily", and was amazed to observe from the

Right: *Cherry Kearton and Theodore Roosevelt.*

train the expanses of grassland and savannah; "further up country, I thought that some of it was very like the English parkland".[7]

It was not just the landscape that caught Kearton unawares. There were creatures roaming across it he couldn't identify, some of them in herds hundreds strong. Their copiousness, on the face of it making the task of the photographer that much the easier, would work against him, as only one member of a herd raising the alarm would put them all to flight. And whereas the gun enabled remote predation from a distance of two hundred yards, the cameraman had to get in close, like a stalking animal, in a landscape with sparse cover. Then there were the sores from grass seed to contend with, and "literally thousands of ticks". His romantic notion of the African night, of sleeping alone with nature, was disillusioned too, the reality being lying awake for hours listening to the "hundred uncomfortable noises" of hyena, jackal, rhinoceros and lion.[8]

Was there was a further obstacle Kearton had to overcome—a cultural one? For the only man on the continent shooting with a cine camera rather than a gun, the social order built around territory and hunting might prove impenetrable. It has been suggested (see for example Jean-Baptiste Gouyon)[9] that in the "Imperial hunting grounds" that existed for the "exclusive enjoyment of a social elite", Kearton would be viewed with suspicion if not hostility, his role dangerously egalitarian, set on sharing African wildlife with broad sections of Western society via the cinema, and promoting Africa as the playground of the animal rather than the hunter. Gouyon suggests that Kearton knew to join forces with American hunters— James L. Clark; Roosevelt and his entourage; Buffalo Jones in 1910; James Barnes in 1913—because in America "access to the land and to the game by means of hunting was open to everyone", and that this "shrewd manoeuvre" could circumvent the existing social order. In practice, there is little evidence that Kearton was cold-shouldered; in terms of nationality, race, gender and politics he was home and dry; he appeared adept at straddling class barriers; and all that remained for him to be accepted as 'one of the men' was to go out with a flash-light after dinner and shoot a few springhares.

It no doubt helped that William Coates was alongside, hunting in his own right, collecting heads and hides to furnish the walls of his London home. This tied in with his role as manager and bodyguard; when attacked by big game, Kearton would avoid red tape if possible by leaving the shooting to his companion, who unlike Kearton had a hunting licence. Lending a semblance of legitimacy and responsibility to the colonialists' appropriation of the wilderness and its

Above: *Plains zebras.*

animal population, the licence literally put a price on animals' heads: £50 for fifty mammals per hunter, with special conditions attached. Additional kills could be had for a levy, the highest premium being placed on the bull elephant, at £17. Extra giraffe and rhino cost £5; antelope £3; other buck, such as wildebeest or waterbuck, £2. No licence was needed for shooting lions and leopards, which were classed as vermin.

The Roosevelts had by this time torn up their original shopping list of a Noah's Ark—or Noah's Morgue—of male and female pairs of each significant species. The field sport of shooting to kill carried its own momentum; Teddy Roosevelt was not one to miss an opportunity, and over the course of the ten-month safari to which he was committed, there would be very many—perhaps too many—opportunities. He was short-sighted and inclined to fire off at whatever moved, until it stopped moving; the homesickness that soon blighted him he medicated with adrenalin and alcohol. Kermit proved such a poor shot ("rank", in Loring's opinion)[10] that many of the quarry were grievously wounded rather than killed outright; most of these were finished off at close quarters, but some slunk away and evaded capture, including at least three wounded hippos that submerged and were not seen again. The number of animals killed or trapped (a small number was captured alive and shipped to American zoos)

Above: *"Flashlight photograph of a maneless African lion"*.

totalled 11,397. According to Theodore Roosevelt's own tally, that figure included about four thousand birds, two thousand reptiles and amphibians, five hundred fishes, and 4,897 mammals (other sources put this figure at 5,103). The smaller prey were mostly collected by the naturalists, while 512 of what are now dubbed 'charismatic megafauna' fell to Theodore's and Kermit's guns, including seventeen lion, eleven elephant, three leopard, seven cheetah, nine hyena, nine white and eleven black rhinoceros, seven hippopotamus, fifteen plains and five Grévy's zebra, seven giraffe, six buffalo and a single crocodile. The expedition consumed the flesh of 262 of the animals. Also taken were marine, land and freshwater shells, crabs, beetles and other invertebrates, not to mention several thousand plants, making a total of 23,151 natural history specimens. A separate collection was made of ethnographic objects. The material took eight years to catalogue.

Roosevelt did his damnedest to justify the bloodbath. Surplus hides and specimens were donated to natural history museums across the USA, enabling him to defend his position with the circular argument: "I can be condemned only if the existence of the National Museum, the American Museum of Natural History, and all similar zoological institutions are to be condemned".[11] What's more, he reasoned, collecting multiple examples of species would enable scientific comparisons to be made. Animal populations had to be kept in check. Shooting lions would save the lives of herbivores. Roosevelt even suggested that he was charitably easing the load on the shoulders of Mother Nature by acting as her agent in matters of destiny: the "normal endings of stately creatures of the wilderness were, if not by violence, then cold or starvation".[12]

Kearton and Coates assembled the provisions for their own modest safari, hired a complement of 14 porters, a soldier, guard, cook and servant, and left for Lake Naivasha on 21 May. They spent two months on and around the lake, securing footage of birdlife but being frustrated by the wariness and nocturnal habits of the larger creatures to get much more than middle-distance shots of hippo in the water. Their plans at this stage appeared no less evasive than the wildlife. There was a motion picture to be made in Africa, for sure; but of what? A conservation message, conveyed in verité shots of African wildlife going about its business, i.e. for the most part grazing or dormant, risked lacking sufficient drama; action shots would test the limits of Kearton's equipment and techniques, while the dangers of provoking big game animals to uncontrolled charges into the camera were more than obvious. To validate the Roosevelt venture as a scientific collecting expedition would demand that Kearton join the retinue, which was never on the cards. There was the further complication that Kearton had expressed his purpose of promoting the idea of the camera safari, and it would have been perverse to have done so by documenting a traditional hunting and collecting expedition—especially this one. The end of July saw them back in Nairobi.

On the first day of August, Kearton set up a meeting with James L. 'Jimmy' Clark, an innovative taxidermist who was collecting skins for his employer, the New York Natural History Museum, and who had recently finished acting as guide and bodyguard to Arthur Radclyffe Dugmore's six-month photo-safari (Dugmore was on a contract from Collier's magazine to secure photos for a series titled 'Snapping Africa's Big Game: The Camera that beat Roosevelt to the Jungle'). Clark offered the mouth-watering information that he had recently been at Sultan Hamud, where he had run into a bunch of fourteen lions. "If there was one thing I desired more than another it was to get moving pictures of lions in their natural state, and the attractions of fourteen of the animals prowling about together were irresistible".[13] On the spot, Kearton agreed to hire Clark and to pay his expenses and those of his men, boy, gun bearer and two porters. (In the event, they failed to find the lions, and were very nearly stampeded by two rhino, one of which Kearton shot dead in self-defence). It was an astute move to hire Clark: William Coates would return home "for business reasons" in mid-August, although it is not clear whether that was known when Clark was hired; it was becoming evident that Kearton could use some real on-the-ground expertise to succeed in filming big game; and the American's zoological credentials and familiarity with Africa might bolster the Kearton project's credibility, not least in the eyes of the president.

The Roosevelt party was also in Nairobi at the end of July, for 'race week'. On 3 August a dinner was held at the Railway Institute for the Americans and their guests, about 180 in all. The following day Roosevelt left for Mount Kenya, and Cherry Kearton went with several others to the station to see him off. While they waited for the train "he took my arm and as we walked up and down the platform, he asked if there was anything he could do to help me. 'Yes', I said. 'You can let me take a few feet of film of you when you get to work'. I hadn't much hope that he would agree; and I was accordingly all the more delighted when after a moment's hesitation he said: 'All right. I will do that for you, Kearton, because you have done so much for natural history'".[14]

But what Roosevelt had in mind was something other than helping Kearton's promotion of natural history by being filmed "getting to work" with it on the trail. A big *ingoma*, or native war dance, had been arranged in Roosevelt's honour by the Acting-Governor of Kenya, Sir Frederick Jackson, for later in the month at Nyeri, and it was agreed "that I should take cinematograph pictures of it and at the same time of Roosevelt watching it. Of course that was exactly what I wanted. The ex-President of the United States of America at a war dance of African natives—what better subject could possibly be sought…!"[15]

For a natural history photographer on his first visit to Africa, who days before had declared his wish-list headed by "moving pictures of lions in their natural state", this was surely Kearton making the best of a bad job. His boyish appetite could, of course, be whetted by whatever slice of cake was placed before him; but it might be that on the preceding evening, Roosevelt himself had unwittingly suggested a new direction for the film. The Colonel, as his preferred title was now, had given a speech on 'Education in Africa', the greater part of it about elucidating white interests in the continent with his own opinions. More expansionist than colonialist, Roosevelt argued for a political and economic stability that he believed would be the reward of the "right type" of settler, who would invest rather

Above: *"The white rhinoceros... alert and suspicious"*.

than speculate in a land of which "very large tracts are fit for a fine population and healthy and prosperous settlements, and it would be a calamity to neglect them... I am convinced that this country has a great agricultural and industrial future..." As for the indigenous population, Roosevelt objected that black people "have not governed themselves and never could", but at least demanded that "the black man be treated with justice, that he be safeguarded in his rights and not pressed downwards. Brutality and injustice are especially hateful when exercised on the helpless".[16]

However his attitude may strike us on our own terms, it was widely reported in America as a modernising speech, viewed in retrospect as contributing towards a changing perception of Africa. Henry M. Stanley's *In Darkest Africa* had been published in 1890, Conrad's *Heart of Darkness* in 1899. Roosevelt's speech was seen as advocating a transition to a new spirit of enlightenment, spelled out some years later in the title of the memoirs of his adviser, Carl Akeley: *In Brightest*

Above: *"Cheetahs are handsome creatures"*.

Africa. By inference, this extended to a change in perceptions of African wildlife, from "nature worthy of fear to nature in need of nurture".[17]

Here was a lifeline, of sorts: if Kearton couldn't have the hunter, he could have the visionary, by turning the direction of the film towards the awakening of the president's imagination to the richness and ripe potential of Africa's Eden. Besides, whatever came of it, Kearton would still have Roosevelt, in Africa, on film, exclusively.

The safaris of Roosevelt, Kearton and Jackson pitched camp at Nyeri on 23 August, and the *ingoma* took place the following day. Kearton filmed Roosevelt breakfasting at camp; planting a ceremonial tree; and examining a presentation gun. He caught the wardance of one thousand Masai in warpaint, and the president watching; reviewing marching manoeuvres; and Masai or Kikuyu women forming a ceremonial circle. The filming ended after some of the official party threw coins to the little girls to bring them in front of the lens, when "there was a veritable stampede towards us, all the children yelling for money simultaneously, and we were practically mobbed by them".[18] Kearton obtained a further concession to record Roosevelt heading out on the trail: on 27 August, he filmed the American camp and Roosevelt with his tent; "we then went up on the bank and got Mr Roosevelt alone on horseback... from here we rushed on in advance of his safari, until we found the ford of the river where the caravan was to cross. Here we placed the camera, in mid-stream, and took the party crossing".[19] Then Roosevelt was gone.

Kearton telegrammed his success back to the UK, where Cherry Kearton Ltd was hastily registered to handle the rights to the Roosevelt footage. He stayed on in Africa until October, capturing on film what further species he could, before sailing home with film reels, souvenirs, a few skins and heads, and his diaries. Bookshop windows would soon be full of impressions penned by the leading figures in the Roosevelt entourage, and Kearton had the march on them all. The story of his trip to Africa, his unique experiences of attempting to film wildlife, meeting the president, and discussing attitudes to hunting, collecting, conservation and nature-faking, would yield more than enough, for a book of greater topical interest than many that would be published; but he held back. Not until a year later did the periodical *Moving Picture World* announce that Kearton "has written a book, to which President Roosevelt kindly supplies the introduction. The book purports to be written by the fox terrier. This is a novel idea and is likely to succeed".[20] Coming so soon after the nature-faking controversy, it seems unlikely that Roosevelt would have had anything to do with something affecting to have been written by a dog. The book did not see light of day. For whatever reason, Kearton's written account missed the boat by about three years, emerging in 1913 as a section of *Photographing Wildlife Across the World*. The volume was dedicated "To my dear friend Theodore Roosevelt".

The usable footage from Africa was sent to Pathé Frères, who edited the 3,000ft or so into a two-reel film, something over 20 minutes in length, with 36 scenes, titled *Roosevelt in Africa*.[21] Since most of it was shot unstaged and without much sense of being part of an overall narrative, it is to the credit of both Kearton and Pathé that *Nickelodeon*, on 1 April 1910, pronounced it a "great feature picture" with sufficient shape to engage an audience. That "shape" was a cobbling-together of footage into a narrative of sorts. Scenes of the Colonel were neatly sandwiched between general views of Mombasa, and shots of the amusements at Luna Park, where we see black

Africans riding on a Ferris wheel, to suggest the president's impressions on making landfall. Footage from the observation platform of a train travelling from Kiu to Nakuru stood for his journey to the interior, where scenes typical of what he might have seen included Masai women and children collecting water at a spring, and drawing water from a well; a rainmaker dancing; a kraal with mud houses; and native boys asking to have their pictures taken. Masai and Kikuyu are shown, both incorrectly identified on the slates throughout as Zulu; probably Pathé's error, although Kearton should have picked it up. Wildlife is represented by a number of scenes of African birds, taken around Naivasha in May and June, including kingfisher, Marabou stork, vulture, a woodpecker and Jackson's widowbird. Back in Roosevelt's company we experience the day of the *ingoma*, before the scene of him setting out on the trail on horseback alerts us to expect more wildlife scenes.

The best—and worst—was saved for last. The *Moving Picture World* picked out for special praise a scene offering "probably the best idea any of us will ever get of how a herd of giraffe look in their native home", and another of hippos at play: "as interesting and correct… as ever was or will be taken. A masterpiece…" But Kearton was roundly criticised for editing in the only shot of a lion he was able to obtain, a tripwire flashlight still taken at night, which "looks like a dead lion, or a poor wash drawing"; so unrealistic did it appear that *Variety* reported it "taken from a painting, or carved animal".[22] The inclusion of a still into the film "casts over the whole series a feeling of patchwork". And for some reason the logical closing shot, of the outspanning safari fording the river, was eclipsed by another dud, a still of Roosevelt in Rough Rider costume, taken ten years previously.

At first sight, it is easy to dismiss the Kearton film as a medley of opportunistic fragments, which would place it within what was becoming a passé cinematic convention, identified by Tom Gunning as the 'cinema of attraction'. This contented itself with the entry-level "matter of making images seen",[23] a substitute for the real thing, cinematic *tableaux vivants* with the music-hall values of variety performance. In fact, it was an odd hybrid that collaged slivers of reality into a fictitious narrative, thoroughly misrepresenting what the world knew of Roosevelt's time in Africa. A more candid title would have been *Kearton in Africa*. Paradoxically, later critical appreciation found this a strength, lauding how the emphasis on realness was balanced against story, and identifying it as a key document

Right: *"Kikuyu with tobacco jar"*.

of the 'transitional' phase of cinema (1909–1917), characterised by contradictions in filmmakers' commitments to fact and to fiction, and by the influence, but not dominance, of narrative. One feature of transitional cinema was the ascendancy of actor over genre: Roosevelt was already a star, now he could be a film star. Indeed, on his return to the States he was filmed so much as to be one of the big screen's earliest celebrities. Roosevelt had achieved much in establishing a sense of American identity; it would be cinema, more than any other medium, which would continue shaping that identity into the 20th century.

Roosevelt in Africa received a private viewing in London on 30 November 1909 at the Alhambra Theatre, but was not released until 18 April 1910, by the Motion Picture Patents Company. The delay was caused perhaps by Kearton, aware of the enormous public curiosity aroused by the safari, trying to sell his negatives at film-star prices, ahead of the game of the Hollywood money-factory. As the *Bioscope* reported on 21 April 1910, he had asked the unprecedented price of $65,000, equivalent to around $1.6 million in today's terms. He did not get it, but did get "a good price, a price that would stagger an ordinary camera man, working on salary and expenses". The 2,000ft film was made available at the high price of 20 cents a foot; *Variety* reported it "without doubt the most expensive negative ever printed from". The licensees releasing the film were criticised for exploitation, but the *Bioscope's* opinion was that they "can't hope to make much profit even at that price, since Kearton got his", concluding that "they slipped one over on [Roosevelt] in Africa".

At the time of its release, the *Moving Picture World* reported on a showing in Elizabeth, New Jersey, where it found the management in a state of "bitter disappointment". One commented, "I can't describe what a frost it is". The journalist, H. F. Hoffman, was "prepared for the worst as the film began", but "as it progressed I found it quite interesting. To be sure the film seemed to be badly obscured in spots, and as it annoyed me I know it annoyed others less forgiving than myself". The cinema manager complained that "the class of people who came there" were expecting "Roosevelt all the way through... slaughtering lions and tigers and wallowing in their gore. They wanted to see a hand-to-hand struggle between him and a white rhinoceros". What they wanted, reasonably enough, was what they had been promised by advertisements that appeared in *Billboard* and elsewhere: "the far-famed American hunter, Colonel Roosevelt, amid

Left: *"Cormorants nesting in a dead tree in Lake Naivasha"*.

the man-eating monsters of the wild African jungle". The sense of grievance that the photographer had failed in his duty to keep track of the guns has persisted: as late as 2011, Ronald B. Tobias, professor of science and natural history filmmaking in the School of Film and Photography at Montana State University, protested that "the film does not include a single hunting scene", under the common misapprehension that "Roosevelt had chosen Kearton" to document the chase.[24]

The success of *Roosevelt in Africa* at the box office was modest compared to the Selig fake of a year before. But Kearton had got what he wanted. He had gone to Africa a British bird photographer and returned an international wildlife film-maker. The income from *Roosevelt in Africa* kick-started a new career and way of life: Kearton shortly became studio proprietor and film director, and spent much of the next five years travelling and filming abroad. He was in New York in 1913 to hear Theodore Roosevelt pronounce: "In moving pictures of wild life there is a great temptation to fake, and the sharpest discrimination must be employed in order to tell the genuine from the spurious. My attention was particularly directed toward Mr Kearton's work because of its absolute honesty. If he takes a picture it may be guaranteed as straight".[25]

Theodore Roosevelt decided in favour of standing again for presidency. He did well in the primaries, but a constitutional regulation prevented him from running for the presidential post for the Republicans. Undeterred, he founded his own political opposition, the National Progressive (or 'Bull Moose') Party, which in the 1912 election beat the Republicans into third place, a unique achievement in American politics. The election was won for the Democrats by Woodrow Wilson.

Many of the Roosevelt animals, mounted by the Smithsonian for exhibition, remained on display for most of the twentieth century. In the late 1950s they were reconditioned for new diorama exhibits. Today, just one expedition specimen is on show: a square-lipped (white) rhinoceros.[26]

Cherry Kearton's pursuit of anthropological subjects, which dated back to photographing St Kildans and English bird-catchers and had been reawakened in Africa in 1909, was revisited the following year in his earliest feature film, *A Primitive Man's Career to Civilisation*. This was something of a faux pas, a no doubt well-intentioned but misguided attempt to demonstrate the benefits of white civilisation by showing African "savages" learning to shave, wear Western

Above: *Filming 'Tembi'.*

clothes, go to church and read and write. It was fairly typical of the received wisdom of its day regarding attitudes to Africa, although stopping short of reverting to the comic stereotyping found in some of Kearton's near-contemporaries, notably Martin and Osa Johnson. (Typical of the charges levelled against the husband-and-wife wildlife film-makers is Eric Barnouw's criticism that their "unabashed condescension and amusement... often express a barely concealed contempt for tribal peoples").[27]

That might have been the end of it, but against the odds Cherry Kearton got it right in 1929 with the film *Tembi*, co-directed by his wife Ada. Based in part on "an old legend of one of the native tribes", this was one of the very earliest films to feature no white people, all parts being played by members of the Wakamba tribe, with no acting experience.[28] The film, which appears now to be effectively lost, has been praised in modern times not merely for its "intention to show a genuine Africa", but as a "pioneering effort to break a perceptual barrier that kept other nonfiction filmmakers from seeing Africans as people".[29]

....

CHAPTER SIX

Deceiving wild creatures

On 24 May 1907, Richard Kearton "got up at 1 a.m. and went out to watch for foxes". He made a note in his diary of the times at which different birds began to sing:

Cuckoo	2.14
Lesser Whitethroat	2.20
Skylark	2.22
Nightjar	2.30
Songthrush	2.45
Blackbird	2.50
Bullfinch	3.15
Robin	3.25
Tree Pipit	3.26
Whitethroat C.	3.30
Rook	3.30
Wryneck	3.35
Chaffinch	4.00

In her autobiography written almost fifty years later, and long after the deaths of both Richard and Cherry, Ada Cherry Kearton wrote that while living in Kenley in the late 1930s, "Cherry conducted some very interesting experiments, noting day after day the exact time that the first notes of each species were heard".[1] Coincidentally, what she selected to publish from "our records" as "a fairly typical day" was another 24 May (year not stated). The first ten singers recorded were:

Cuckoo	3.16
Lesser Whitethroat	3.22
Skylark	3.24
Songthrush	3.47
Blackbird	3.52
Bullfinch	4.17
Robin	4.27
Tree Pipit	4.28
Common Whitethroat	4.32
Chaffinch	5.02

Left: *Nightingale.*

Crucially, the records for nightjar, rook and wryneck that appear in Richard's 1907 field diaries were omitted when he published the list in October of that year in *The Fairyland of Living Things*.[2] That leaves us with the same ten songbirds, singing in the same order, in each case starting exactly one hour and two minutes later in Cherry's records than in Richard's. The one hour difference is accounted for by the introduction of daylight saving time in 1916. One is left wondering how conceivable it is that these identical species—perhaps not all of them the most regular of garden visitors—and no others, sang in the environs of both Richard's house, on the valley floor between the road and railway line, and Cherry's relatively isolated villa in its woodland setting on top of the downs; all in the same order, all two minutes later than thirty years previously; and that Cherry did not hear, or failed to record, the three species that Richard had chosen to discount.

If we conclude that this is a coincidence too far, the most immediate explanation seems to be that Cherry was innocently employing a little trick to amuse and entertain his wife, not knowing that she would go on to publish it. But if that were the case, why did he go so far as to advance Richard's times by two minutes? Was he capable of exercising similar strategies, and trying to smear the traces, when it came to amusing and entertaining his public?

Conveniently, we can begin to test his susceptibility to hyperbole by comparing like with like. His first book, *Wild Life Across the World*, was a relatively sumptuous volume covering the early international expeditions: the 'Roosevelt' safari of 1909; the back-to-back 'lasso-ing' and 'lion-spearing' safaris of 1910; Borneo and India, 1911; and Canada and Yellowstone Park, 1912. The book was republished in 1923 in a revised edition as *Photographing Wild Life Across the World*, which added new chapters on time spent in East Africa during 1915–18, and in South Africa and the Congo in 1921, to "about two-thirds" of the original volume, "rewritten and carefully edited".[3]

In the interim, Kearton had been divorced and remarried, so it is perhaps not surprising that the rewriting and editing should have removed a 3,500-word section of the diary of his first wife Mary, describing how she nursed him from a fever so extreme that Kearton believed that, but for her "unceasing care and tenderness", he would not have survived. The excision of this renders ironic Kearton's assertion that her attentions were "one of the things a man does not forget, a memory to treasure always".[4] Some other rewriting is innocuous, for example "monkey" lately identified as "loris" and "Dancing Bird" as "Jackson's Dancing Bird";[5] the manpower of the

Above: *"The lion"*.

lassoing safari was revised downwards drastically—and a little mystifyingly—from eleven Europeans to seven, "some three hundred natives" to one hundred, and fifteen horses to just seven. Much of the original text is left untouched; however, several passages, including one relating the spearing of a lion, during which Kearton's dog Simba joined in and apparently bit the lion's tail, are heavily rewritten with added portions of melodrama. Nothing wrong with that, if Kearton believed his original failed to do justice to the danger and excitement of the hunt. But in places we begin to suspect that something more than flair is being added.

The original report, for example, that lions were near the camp, and "we waited till nine o'clock in the hope of their being found, then struck camp, and trekked on"[6] becomes a rather different scene: "failing to locate any of the brutes, gave up the quest about nine o'clock. On returning, we found the camp in commotion and boys up trees, as a rhino had just galloped through... we struck camp and moved on quickly".[7] In a book in which Kearton is sometimes reduced to acknowledge that "on the whole, from the naturalist's point of view, the trip was a barren one",[8] this seems an odd omission. Similarly, the newly-remembered detail that when the lion broke cover, "he had to pass my camera-boy and dog. For a second he paused within

Above: *"The first and possibly the only photograph ever taken of a Masai lion hunt"*.

twelve yards to have a look…";[9] and a new passage describing how Kearton was told that in the final moments of the hunt "The lion has killed a Masai… I certainly saw the leg of a Masai against the body of the lion, and concluded my dog was dead as well…",[10] surprisingly not thought worth mentioning in the original publication. The added detail smoothes the way for a polished denouement, in which we learn that the recumbent Masai had speared the lion clean through the heart, "dived in to get the tip of the tail, as this constitutes ownership of the skin and mane; but the dog had hold of it first, and when he had attempted to take it away she had bitten him".[11]

It is hard to reconcile some other changes with Kearton's later assertion that "I have never permitted myself to write even the slightest exaggeration of actual fact".[12] The information given originally that at a Masai kraal, two lions "had passed within four or five hundred yards only ten minutes before"[13] is in the later version deceptively rendered as "two man-eating lions… were so cheeky that they were within five hundred yards *of where we stood* [my italics]… Two lions so near—think of it!"[14] This casual ramping-up of tension at the expense of accuracy comes out of kilter from one of whom a companion, the Hon. Berkeley Cole, was reported to say that "during all the years he has been in Africa he has never seen any one go so near a lion and show so little fear".[15] Equally dubious is Kearton's rewriting of what happened to the second lion. In the original account, "the Somalis were anxious to keep both the animals, but, as we could not tackle the two simultaneously, we decided to let one escape"; the lioness then "went off, the moment she had the chance..."[16] This is replaced by a scene in which the Masai advanced, "spears poised in the air, daring the lion and lioness to come out... then a strange thing happened. The lioness bolted. I afterwards found out that she had dashed at a Somali who had ventured too near..."[17]

What makes this geeing-up especially unfortunate is that it carries so little advantage, the events being thrilling enough already. The origins of it are hinted at in a revelation in the autobiography of Cherry's wife Ada, *On Safari*. After his doctor had advised Cherry to lead a more sedentary life while recuperating from a bout of ill-health in 1925, Ada bought a typewriter and suggested "he should dictate a book about his adventures with animals".[18] At first "he flatly refused; but eventually I persuaded him to tell me a number of stories about Toto, his favourite chimpanzee; and these I surreptitiously typed out". In her recollection, Ada presented Cherry with "several hundred typewritten sheets", and said: "Do link them up to make a book. Children would love them" (the 'them' suggesting she was intending more than one book). Given Kearton's willingness to lean on the words of other authors (witness the pages-long passages borrowed from J. H. Fabre, March Phillips and the Rev. J. G. Wood in *The Shifting Sands of Algeria*), it is conceivable that, as far as possible, he would have left Ada's words to speak for themselves.

There is evidence for thinking that Ada's input into Cherry's writing may not have begun or ended there. She had an editorial claim on some of her husband's books, rewriting with revisions, for example, the 1930 title *The Island of Penguins* as *Penguin Island* in 1960. The introduction and four of the original chapters were shredded entirely, and the remainder tightened up. Four of Kearton's pet books from the 1920s—*Simba, Toto, My Animal Friendships* and *My Happy Chimpanzee*—were similarly rewritten and gathered into a single volume, *The Cherry Kearton Animal Book*, which was published in 1958 with, oddly, no author named on the title page, and the copyright to Ada Cherry Kearton. It is not hard to detect in these books traces of her writing style, demonstrated in *On Safari* and her novel, *Under African Skies*. There is a tendency to break blocks of text into shorter paragraphs, with the characteristic tic of detaching the first sentence and setting it as a stand-alone paragraph. The style tends to be more pacey than Cherry's and scattered with more reported speech, the collation of stark fact into fluent narrative suggestive of one for whom the fruit of experience was its conversion to compelling anecdote.

Might Ada's typewriter have arrived as early as 1923, and been put to work in the makeover of *Photographing Wild Life Across the World*? One reason for thinking this might be so comes from *On Safari*, in which Ada wrote that of Cherry's "early adventures in Africa I need say little, for in later years we enjoyed together the delights of many safaris, similar to those of his early visits".[19] But further into the book she was unable to resist retelling, with all the detail of her husband's account and some new flourishes, the stories of Cherry's adventures with a charging rhino, the Masai lion hunt and a later maned lion hunt—stories that had been subject of the most drastic revisions of 1923. Could she have been their original editor, as well as narrator of his raciest adventures? A pointer in this direction is the curious inclusion in *On Safari* of a lengthy description of Cherry's ascent in an airship over London in 1908. Curious, because it was not part of her experience of his life, and was not central to his career as a nature photographer. But it is almost all of what we learn from Ada about Cherry's life in the rich, formative years 1895–1908.

Kearton had seen the potential to publicize the endeavours of the film company to which he was then contracted, as well as those of his "old friends" the Spencer aeronaut family and—not least—himself, by re-enacting the first airship flight over St Paul's Cathedral, which had been made by Stanley Spencer in his *Airship No.2* on 17 September 1903. He contacted Percival Spencer, who had inherited brother Stanley's interests on his death in 1906, and it was agreed Kearton would fly with the Spencers. The aerial film of London that he took would be dropped onto the roof of Urbanora House, Charles Urban's film studios in Wardour Street that had opened the previous month, and be shown in West End cinemas that evening.

According to Kearton, the ascent took place on 4 May, although contemporary newspaper reports show that it was 1 May. The airship, which seems to have been a composite of the triangular-section bamboo gondola of Stanley Spencer's *Airship No.1* with a new engine and envelope, was readied at Wandsworth Gas Works, coal gas being the cheapest available lifting agent (£5, compared with £50 to inflate the envelope with hydrogen). A substantial crowd waved it off at 3 p.m., with three on board: Percival Spencer's sons—Herbert at the controls and Henry as engineer—and Cherry Kearton with his film camera.

Above: *"Elephant contemplating a charge".*

In Kearton's breathless narrative, which saw light of day in *Adventures with Animals and Men*,[20] the "first excitement" came at once, with the airship narrowly avoiding the roof of a building; at "between three and four thousand feet up" the engine began to backfire, and then the vessel "suddenly heeled over, canted on one side, seemed to think of turning round and then to decide against it. At one second the nose pointed upwards, at the next it pointed downwards". It dropped "so that we were threatened with a sudden descent on to the London roofs", and when some of the sandbag ballast had been released "with extraordinary swiftness we rose" into the clouds. Soon, the engine "started a series of explosions", while there was a strong smell of gas "let out to counteract our sudden rise". The engine stopped, due to a broken petrol pipe, and "I expected immediate disaster. By all the rules, we ought to have gone up in a sheet of flame and then to have tumbled, charred and unrecognizable, to the earth". They had by then "reached a height of fourteen thousand feet. My nose was bleeding and I felt the hammering of piston-rods in both my ears". The airship "swung giddily round and round as if caught in a whirlpool… for a second we hung uncer-

Above: *Spencer Brothers' airship ascending at Wandsworth Gas Works, 1 May 1908.*

tainly—and then we dropped. Straight through the clouds we went, down, down, down, and I had a sensation like that of the nightmare in which one falls headlong and horribly over the edge of a cliff". Spencer gesticulated for Kearton to drop the ballast of his camera overboard, but it was lashed to the gondola basket so instead "since I am incurably an optimist, I thought that perhaps I shouldn't be killed after all and in that event I had now an absolutely unique opportunity of securing pictures". He was reportedly still filming when "the nose of the framework hit the ground, twisting the tubing of the propeller and burying it in the ground. Bamboo poles broke and splintered... we were thrown off our feet and fell into a confusion of bamboo and tubing and pipes, with the gasbag all on top of us; but we scrambled out unhurt..."

Contemporary reports are rather less giddy. In Herbert Spencer's words, at the start of the flight: "Rising to a fair height the ship was first put through a number of evolutions over the ground, which proved its ability to travel in any direction". The engine transpiring to be inadequate in the face of a mild 12–15mph wind, the attempt to reach St Paul's was abandoned. When the petrol pipe fractured, according to one report "Mr Spencer had some difficulty with the motor at the outset of the voyage, but put it right at considerable personal risk".[21] The airship reached a maximum altitude of 8,000 feet—hardly enough to cause the reported symptoms of altitude sickness—and drifted south over Streatham and Norwood towards Croydon, where it landed near Factory Lane, by Croydon Electric Light Company, at about 5pm. Newspapers reported the airship "bumping on the ground";[22] but a *London Daily News* reporter at the site observed "the ship was eventually brought to the ground without mishap",[23] while Herbert Spencer, interviewed on the same day by the *Daily Chronicle*, described how: "the descent was very easy. As we came slanting downwards two or three men caught the rope and held us down. Then we made another short experimental ascent, and circled round the field before the thousands of people who quickly gathered. Then we came down for good, and in a short time everything was packed on a Pickford's van and on its way back to our balloon works at Highbury... Everything is in perfect order and we could make another ascent tomorrow—in fact I wish we were going to".[24]

The escapade was not mentioned in Richard's litany of Cherry's mishaps and lucky escapes in his introduction to *Wild Life Across the World*, and there is no record of Cherry himself referring to it until 1935. But having waited twenty-seven years to tell the story, within a few months he was changing it. In an interview for the *Sydney Morning Herald* of 6 January 1936, during his visit to Australia, it is reported of his "fall in a wrecked dirigible from a height of 10,000 feet", that "it was only by good fortune, Mr Kearton said... that the dirigible turned over in the air when falling, giving the soft cushion of a half-inflated gas-bag to break the occupants' fall", an elaboration that is as implausible as it is untrue. When Ada came to write the story up in *On Safari*, she followed the original account blow by blow, as she had done with the lion hunt stories, but coloured it with some new embellishments: the building narrowly missed became "a large warehouse"; the hammering in Cherry's head occurred at 10,000 feet, and the nose-bleed at 14,000 feet; on crash-landing the airship "struck a hedgerow, glanced off and cartwheeled into a ploughed field".[25]

The story, as told by Cherry and again by Ada, has been repeated many times in print and has become part of the Kearton folklore. Perhaps we need to recognise 'folklore' as just that. There is no doubt that in Cherry Kearton's writing we find inconsistency, exaggeration and obfuscation. It seems that he was unable to resist altering facts to make a more enthralling story, and the evidence is strong that in this he was abetted by Ada Kearton who typed up his verbal dictation, was substantial author of some of the books published in his name, and contributed to parts of others. What is frustrating is that this leaves the perfectly candid majority of his recollections tainted with doubt and suspicion, and the unhappy legacy of the key to vetting his work being that the duller the writing, the more likely it is to be authentic. If this appears unfair, there remains a puzzling gulf between the qualities of penmanship found in, for example, the fluent after-dinner chattiness of *My Woodland Home* and the laborious *Cherry Kearton's Travels*; and what to make of the unexpected fable *In the Land of the Lion*, with its sudden access to more metaphor and simile than all his other books together?

This raises one other possibility for the origins of the 'fake' records of birdsong times described at the start of this chapter: that the times were adjusted by Ada, perhaps to heap as much credit on the shoulders of her deceased beloved as they would take. Cherry Kearton himself makes no claim to have made such records, and even quotes Richard's original observations—with times unaltered—in *My Woodland Home*, written at about the time (1937–38) Ada described him making his "interesting experiments". It would surely have been futile for him to have attempted the harmless deception on Ada, as suggested above, while simultaneously publishing the truth. How and why the suspect list with altered times came to be written, and by whom, is likely to remain a mystery; but we know it was done carelessly, Ada's account recording sunrise at 3:58 a.m., the pre-day-light savings time, uncorrected from Richard's original.

Cherry was at times impatient of the writer's obligation to plain fact, excusing himself with, for example, "Mombasa is too well known now for me to attempt to describe it" in *Wild Life Across the World*,[26] while his reliance on lengthy quotations from other authors, in for example *The Shifting Sands of Algeria*, is noted above. Cherry's fastidiousness at crediting his sources stopped short when it came to his own brother; suffice to say, examples of his unacknowledged borrowing from Richard's writing are not hard to find. On the subject of birds' nests, for example, Richard wrote "some feathered builders are miners, others plasterers, carpenters, weavers, raft-builders and scaffold makers, and a few do not trouble to make any kind of home at all". Compare this to Cherry's "amongst the feathered builders there are the equivalents of miners, plasterers, carpenters, weavers,

Right: *"Female yellowhammer feeding young"*.

raft-builders, and scaffolders, whilst in contrast others do not trouble to make any homes at all". Or again, in the same sources,[27] Richard notes "the Song Thrush, which has been known to pour forth his music for sixteen hours out of the twenty-four, occasionally practises in an undertone, as if doing it only for his own amusement"; while Cherry offers "as I have said, the song-thrush has been known to perform vocally for sixteen out of the twenty-four hours, occasionally practising in an undertone... whether it was done for practice or amusement I never discovered..."

*

"Never in the whole of my varied photographic career have I faked a picture."—Cherry Kearton, *My Woodland Home*[28]

In 2009, the winner of the Natural History Museum's prestigious Veolia Environment Wildlife Photographer of the Year competition, José Luis Rodriguez, was obliged to return his £10,000 award when his close-up photograph of a supposedly wild Iberian wolf leaping a gate was recognised as having been shot in a wildlife park near Madrid, the wolf being a trained animal available for hire named Ossian. Among nature photographers, this has gone into modern mythology as the archetype of bad practice, but it is nothing new: the filming and photography of captive specimens, and attempting to pass them off as the real thing, has been with us since Kearton's time and before, as we have seen from the fake Selig film purportedly showing Roosevelt shooting a lion. Among naturalists, it is considered a crime of the highest order, and not without reason: photography and film are a first resource of naturalists and conservationists for the understanding of appearance, behaviour and population, and actions taken on the evidence of a single faked shot can waste time, misdirect funds, and damage reputations. This is much more so the case now than it was then; but it matters that Kearton was vociferous and categorical in denying that he had ever done such a thing.

The precise definition of what makes a 'faked' picture is debatable but, by the standards that saw Rodriguez disqualified, we can say that any attempt to pass off a shot of an animal in captivity as 'wild' crosses the line. An instance of Kearton appearing to be guilty of just this occurs in *Wild Life Across the World*, in which he published his

Left: *"It's my turn now, brother Billy".*

diary entry for 7 August 1909: "There were plenty of lions about, we were told, so we made an early start the following day. However, we saw nothing of the animals, and we did not manage to get within photographic range of any of the other game. In the afternoon I had better luck, securing pictures of the red colobus monkey..." The diary of his companion on the trip, James L. Clark, tells us what Kearton had not: "In the afternoon Kearton took pictures of a lizard and the red colobus monkey, *which is a pet on a claim here...*" [my italics].[29]

As a 12-year-old boy in 1930, nature film-maker Eric Ashby "watched the great traveller and pioneer of animal photography Cherry Kearton present a public showing of his films about Africa at the South Parade Pier, Portsmouth. Although amused and thrilled by the showman, Ashby detected that not all the animals were behaving naturally..."[30] Since then, numerous commentators have suggested that everything might not be quite right with some of Kearton's scenes. In recent years, technological advances have enabled a more forensic analysis of a number of clips, seemingly confirming what Ashby suspected. In *Nation on Film—Kearton's Wildlife* (BBC, 2005), a Kearton close-up of a male lion drinking was examined by award-winning wildlife cameraman Gavin Thurston, who came to the conclusion that the animal was a tame one. The sequence of the maned lion spearing hunt of 1910 was also picked apart, by Martin Elsbury, editor for the BBC of numerous David Attenborough features, who deduced from the behaviour of the lion that it could only have been tethered.

Kearton wrote up the lion hunt in *Wild Life Across the World*. He had been joined by his wife Mary "after the close of the game-lassoing trip", and they trekked from Kijabe to Berkeley Cole's camp, two days beyond Nyeri across the Aberdare range, "in the hope of securing some moving pictures of lion-spearing". Lions, in general, were classed as vermin and were excluded from the hunting restrictions imposed by licensing conditions governing safaris; the lions in this particular area, Kearton informs us, "were very bad ones, well-known man-eaters", so we are well primed to put aside any qualms about what might otherwise seem *de facto* unwarranted bloodshed. In the late stages of recuperating from fever, Kearton was at a lake fishing when "a Somali came galloping in", with news that a lion had been found by some of his fellow horsemen, who were "holding him up" about five miles away. It took Kearton two hours to return to camp, partake of a quick snack, and proceed to the scene of action, where he found the Somalis had the creature "well in hand". He recorded that the lion was "raging at his enemies"; Kearton's

Above: *"Stroking an eider duck on her nest"*.

observation that he was "puzzled at the number of them, and did not know which way to turn" creates a mental picture of the lion making abrupt movements this way and that. One of the Somalis began taunting the lion by pelting it with small stones; when the lion sprang at him, "it looked as if he must land fairly on the horse, just behind the saddle, but, at the psychological moment, the animal swerved, and escaped with a light scratch".[31]

Was the lion already tethered? Did the Somali act so recklessly knowing that it would not be able to reach his horse? The lion's inability to find its target was repeated a few moments later, when it sprang from cover, having been struck by two spears, and made straight for the camera; then "something seemed to tell him that I was not the real enemy, and he wheeled round to charge the Masai". Kearton appears almost to give the game away in what happened next: the Masai spearmen had formed up behind a line of shields, which the lion charged "from end to end... scratching at them with his huge paw, in one or two instances biting clean through them. Yet not a man moved. *Mad to think he could not reach his foes*, the lion stood, roaring even more hideously than before" [my italics].[32]

Above: *"Masai warriors on the look-out for a man-eating lion".*

Any hint we might read into this that the lion was in some way constrained in his frustrated attempt to "reach his foes" was gone from the revised account of the escapade published in 1923. The wheeling round, the charging, the scratching and biting of the shields, the men in a line not moving—all were thrown to the wind. Instead, we are offered the alarming but relatively vague new information that the lion "quickly put two Masai warriors out of action", charged again and "knocked down another Masai". Despite these three apparent casualties, the conclusion—after the animal had been speared to death—was oddly enough identical in both accounts: that "with the exception of a flesh wound and one or two superficial scratches, no one was really hurt".[33]

There can be no doubt, from Martin Elsbury's investigation, that the lion was tethered; this being the case, Kearton must have known about it. We know that he had been disappointed that he had "not been able to take photographs, owing to the lack of light"[34] of the earlier Simba lion hunt; and that the fever that had subsequently beset him must have raised the possibility of the venture being called off, before achieving its objective. We know, too, that on the Kearton-

Jones expedition, only a few weeks earlier, he had participated in the successful lassoing of a lioness. These facts together add up to little more than conspiracy theory, and at this distance we cannot know what really happened. But there is enough to make credible this hypothesis: that it was arranged by someone in the camp, perhaps Kearton or Cole, that the Somalis would tether a lion, most probably by a hind leg, in the Europeans' absence, and no more would be said about it. There was then more than enough opportunity—time in which a messenger was despatched to camp and redirected to where Kearton was fishing, with the additional two hours for Kearton to return to camp, eat his snack and reach the scene—for the Somali horsemen to test the limits of the tether, and mark the safety zone for the Masai spearmen.

In the weeks before the hunt, Kearton had been "so ill… that my recollection… is very vague", so the published account in *Wild Life Across the World* of this period is the unedited diary of his wife Mary. What is significant here is that the portion of the diary reproduced, purportedly to "fill up the break in the sequence of my story", covered the period from 3 to 22 May 1910. The maned lion spearing hunt, having occurred on the 21st, appears twice: firstly in Mary's words, then in Cherry's. By including both, Cherry conveniently corroborates the detail that he was miles from the scene when the lion was run to ground, and can have had no direct involvement in its being tethered.[35]

A sympathetic reading of Kearton's actions would be that he believed what he had secured on film by fair means had failed to do justice to the actuality of wildlife in Africa, and if he had to resort to sleight of hand to recreate an on-screen equivalent of his genuine experiences, it was to ensure that neither he nor his audience would be disappointed. But of course this could never be admitted; the revisions to his second account of the hunt suggest that accusations of fakery had already been raised, and he found himself obliged for the sake of his reputation to try to play down any indication of abnormality in the lion's behaviour. As far as he was concerned, it would appear, the ruse was successful, for as he wrote in 1923: "The picture just described has been seen on the screen by millions of people, and considered by the greatest hunters the most graphic record in existence".[36]

CHAPTER SEVEN

The wildness of wild life

Nature, as it appears to us through the work of the Keartons, has two faces. One is the inviolable and wonderful structure subject to our unending interrogation, the "tonic of wildness" of which Thoreau wrote: "...we require that all things be mysterious and unexplorable, that land and sea be indefinitely wild, unsurveyed and unfathomed by us because unfathomable. We can never have enough of nature".[1] We elevate it as a world apart from and coexisting with human civilisation, with laws and secrets of its own, complex, fascinating and infinite in its subtleties; a place threatened by mankind, whose cruelty and destructiveness may only be countered by education and understanding. It is what we are invited to imagine by some of the Keartons' titles: *Wild Nature's Ways*, or *Wonders of Wild Nature*. One thinks of a raw and combative arena, a place beyond the reaches. We might note that a near contemporary of the Keartons, photographer Oliver G. Pike, coined a specific nomenclature for the parallel territory of his own investigations: 'Birdland'.

The inference is that the Keartons, through persistence and diligence, have found a way in, and offer us the privilege of sharing their experiences at arm's length via the proxy of their books and photographs. This is as near as we, the uninitiated, are allowed; the territory of 'wild nature' vanishes once humans are detected within its frontiers, our contagion of fear and anxiety lethal to the expression of natural behaviour among creatures going about their business. The Keartons make explicit the ingenuity and complexity of preparation demanded for crossing over, in interventions such as the stuffed ox. This was likened by Richard Kearton to the Trojan Horse, manifestly intended to smuggle them behind the lines; spying on nature, unseen and unknown, they could file their copy from an Eden from which base humanity is banished. It was an illusion of course, more than a deceit; without a reporter, there can be no report.

The other facet of nature lies on the cultural spectrum, in a coexistence of the sacred and the profane. In the Keartons' work there is much interaction with 'the dark side', in which they acted not only

Left: *"Male mute swan sitting on the nest".*

as agents of conservation, to maintain and promote diversity, but also and less obviously to affect natural transactions; to tame some of the wildness they found; to advance the more domestic and civilised aspects of what they observed; and to demonstrate, explicitly or otherwise, moral values. The Keartons played their part in helping define attitudes towards nature in their lifetimes; to understand them tells us something about the apprehension of the natural world then, and helps establish how our awareness and stewardship of it has evolved since. Attitudes have changed; there can be few naturalists today, for instance, who would fire a revolver from the top of a cliff "in the face of which there is reason for believing some bird's nest, which we desire to photograph, is situated, so that by frightening its owner off we may locate the exact spot at which to make a descent".[2]

On the face of it, they were conservationists with a mission to promote hunting with the camera instead of the gun, a "new form of sport" that "possesses the additional advantage of yielding permanent trophies of the skill and endurance of its votaries, whilst leaving the originals to enjoy their wild free lives".[3] The presentation of nature photography as a kind of sport is recurrent: "To pit one's skill and ingenuity against the shyness and cunning of a wild bird, or summon the courage and endurance to descend to its home in the face of some dizzy ocean cliff, is in itself a feat which calls forth the very best hunting instincts of the human race".[4] So the photograph becomes a means of "taming", by securing from nature a photographic trophy, equivalent of the hunter's spoil.

The advance of nature photography was more or less simultaneous with the burgeoning conservation movement. The Society for the Protection of Birds had been founded in 1889 in protest at the destruction of birds for their plumes, which as fashion accessory signalled the descent of high Victorianism into *fin-de-siècle* decadence. The more catholic goal of stopping the wanton slaughter of birds became the founding principle of the society's later chartership as the RSPB. In America, the immediate predecessor of the National Audubon Society came about in a similar way and about the same time. Photography and conservation have since enjoyed a symbiotic relationship: the camera is invaluable to the conservationist, for education, fund-raising and the collection of evidential data, as well as for its role in the battle against poaching. It is a potent tool, which progress in communications media has enabled to get the message across ever more urgently and to an ever expanding audience. Its endowment with the power of truth has been its great asset, and also

Above: *"Common trout... an almost imperceptible current"*.

its weakness, leaving it prone to abuse by selectivity and the outright hoaxes of staged photography.[5] As an alternative to the specimen, the photograph is politically endowed with the democratizing bonus of making the wildest creatures, from the remotest corners of the planet, available and tangible to one and all.[6]

Like most naturalists of his era, Richard Kearton maintained a substantial collection of birds' eggs and stuffed birds, which he considered a valuable reference resource; much of the descriptive part of *British Birds' Nests* was "written from my own specimens... giving, of course, in the case of the birds themselves, due care to the parts that fade and alter after death".[7] While opposing over-collection, in the 1890s he promoted egg-collecting as a healthy and educational hobby, advocating the responsible harvesting of not more than one egg per nest, an enlightened conservation measure for the time (later in life, his advice to would-be collectors was to "try old china or worm-eaten furniture, and give the poor birds a chance").[8] In 1895, he defined his position as that of "a bird lover and collector for more than twenty years", who fully recognised "the immense value, from an educational point of view, of a collection of stuffed birds, especially when set up with the life-like actuality of South Kensington".[9]

As far as the birds themselves were concerned, Richard argued: "...it is difficult to understand why, from a purely national [point of

Above: *"Viper or adder".*

view], we have never given any practical attention to the effective preservation of the infinitely more interesting and precious living creatures themselves".[10] He wrote eloquently of the conservation of the rarer species, and urged that "all who can" should "try to save the few species most in danger, and keep a watchful eye on the reduction of others that are from some cause or other on the decline; for once a bird drops below a certain point of rarity, the premium upon its skin and eggs appears to seal its doom. Let us not forget that we owe posterity a debt, and that the deliberate doing of anything calculated to lessen its pleasure is a wicked responsibility".[11]

In fact, Kearton's expressed attitude was that the Wild Bird Protection laws were "all but unenforceable" and very like "a beautiful padlock and chain, hanging useless on a widely-opened stable door which it is nobody's business to lock"; that the majority of sportsmen were "good field naturalists" who were unfairly abused for the loss of a number of predatory birds, and that creatures such as the golden eagle were "really in no danger at all".[12] This was despite some well-publicised evidence to the contrary, such as the case of the passenger pigeon in North America, once perhaps the world's most numerous bird, whose population of several billion declined by hunting throughout the nineteenth century to reach extinction in 1914. Closer to home, the last great auk was killed in 1844, while the same century saw the extinction of enough breeding populations in the British Isles to cause alarm: the great bustard around 1840, the northern hawk owl around 1860, the black tern in 1885, the great bittern the following year, with the white-tailed eagle to follow early in the twentieth century.

One way of promoting the notion of a tame, benevolent nature was by freelance conservation and culling, and Richard maintained the duties of a gamekeeper learned in the Dales long after he had moved south. In his Surrey diaries, he records shooting crows and magpies, and killing adders, as pests. He joined parties shooting for partridges, especially during the privations of the First World War, and would also go ferreting for rabbits for the pot. According to the tally of his diaries, he caught and took home, presumably for pets, uncounted toads, eight slowworms, a couple of grass snakes and a dozen adders. This last figure at least is likely to be conservative, as his son Cherry remembered that "adders were particularly numerous and on one occasion we caught five in one day. We used to bring them home to Ashdene and take pictures of them on the lawn either stationary or striking at a glove on the end of a stick".[13] In 1921 Richard recorded removing "for cage pets" a brood of fledgling jays, which he believed "make very interesting pets and with a little patience can be taught to talk". This despite his warning that "keeping wild birds in cages… is not a practice to be encouraged, unless it is the only way to save the unfortunate creatures from the wrath of the gamekeeper or the gardener".[14] He seems to have regretted the introduction of the little owl into the UK in the 1880s, noting in his 1920 diary that: "The small bird life is much worse in the Caterham district than I have ever known it to be in 20 years… this is due I think to Little Owls and schoolboys".[15] In 1919, he captured four of the species (owls, not schoolboys), and took them to London Zoo.

Significantly, the Keartons' diversion in the late 1890s into recording the pursuits and practices of country people centred on the capturing and taming of birds for economic purposes. We discover St Kilda folk, with their unique subsistence of seabirds, trapping and netting puffins and fulmars; Yorkshire poachers after moorland game; sparrow catchers at work coaxing nesting birds from a hay rick; and shadowy men on the South Downs luring song birds to be sold as cage pets.[16] In *With Nature and a Camera*, Richard described in some detail the essentials for the successful operation of the duck-decoy, the "most interesting and the most deadly" of contrivances for the capture of wildfowl. The practice was in decline, but the subject of Richard's researches, who worked three "pipes", succeeded one winter in killing 1,500 head of wildfowl. The most important of the "essentials", Kearton believed, was "a man of more than average industry, intelligence, and skill".[17]

It is notable that the first Kearton book was devoted to birds' nests and eggs, the domestic architecture and living art of the avian world. It is not only that these complex and formal structures seem to reach out from the 'wildness' of their origins towards our sentient world. The way the brothers composed their photographs enhances the experience of an adaptation of wild nature to pictorial composition; the "gardening" of the foreground is in effect a parallel for how gardens are a taming of nature, the resemblance of the photographs to the painterly still lifes of Victorian parlours recalling the historic tradition of immortalising the bounty of gathering and harvesting from garden or field. Similarly, we might symbolise the stuffed ox as an exemplar of the go-between; just as that other fabulous hybrid, the satyr, the spirit of the woods, enabled our (or rather the Greeks') understanding of a nature alienated from human intelligence, so the stuffed ox became a latter-day 'spirit of the meadows', connecting the cultivated with the untamed. It was, as we have seen, the product of taxidermist Rowland Ward, living symbol of the translation of wild beast into household ornament.

There is frequent reference, some of it subliminal, to a nature that is more comfortable than wild (one might note the odd comment Cherry made at the start of the lassoing safari: "There is plenty of work for these cooks and personal boys when the white men are doing things comfortably, and, after all, why should one not study comfort?").[18] Richard Kearton's daily field studies were made, year in and year out, on the suburban fringes, in gardens, pastures and hedgerows near his Surrey home. His books for children about single species settle on the seemingly familiar and unthreatening, reinforcing the child's view of a benign nature where rabbits are cuddly and robins friendly. The experiments he undertook with the opening and closing of flowers pick on the homely weed types: dandelion and daisy. His photographs of "curiosities from wild nature" reveal a fascination with birds' nests in human habitation and farmyard situations: robins nesting in discarded biscuit boxes, jam jars and coffee pots; swallows in an old shoe; a blackbird in a tin can; a red-legged partridge under a broken flower pot; a great tit in a disused water pump; a wren in a coil of rope. Other photographic series emphasize the benign, nurturing aspects of nature that reinforce our notions of civilisation as revealed in the family unit and social imperative: witness the caption of one of his most popular photographs showing

Above: *"Sparrow catchers"*.

two great tits on a coconut, "It's my turn now, brother Billy" (see
p.140), or the numerous manifestations of fluffy fledglings cuddled
together. It is hard to ignore the insistence of book titles such as *Baby
Birds at Home, At Home with Wild Nature,* or *Wild Life at Home.*

We can see the distance from our own modern sensibilities in the
proprietorial attitudes the Keartons sometimes took. In 1902, Richard
experimented with wooden songthrush's eggs (made by a local joiner
and painted by Ellen), taking real eggs out of the nest and putting
wooden ones in: "…but as she flew off I noticed something drop—it

Above: *"Hen chaffinch hanged by a hair".*

was one of my wooden eggs which had stuck to her on account of the varnish being warmed by the heat of the bird's body. The other wooden egg had stuck to her altogether under her wing and so feared her that she never came back and I had to take her eggs and give them out to two sitting Blackbirds".[19] In another example of what current legislation might consider interference too far, in 1907 he "took a Robin's own 4 eggs out of nest and replaced them by two Common Sparrows' eggs one Bullfinch's and one Whitethroat's and went into hiding to see what would happen. Directly Robin came back she hopped into nest and sat down without taking the slightest notice of the change".[20]

The most literal index of the collision of nature with culture is the chapter devoted to "strange accidents to wild birds" published in *At Home with Wild Nature*. In this ornithological chamber of horrors we learn of birds dashing themselves against lighthouses, striking telegraph wires or snaring on ships' rigging; of swallows flying into the wheels of bicycles in motion, or being struck down by cricket and golf balls. One report is of a friend of Richard's witnessing partridges colliding with an express train in Lincolnshire, another of a Welsh train being brought to a standstill by a flock of starlings. Nestling birds are found strangled by horse-hair, pieces of string and blades of grass; cockles clamped to the bill of a dunlin and the toe of a greenfinch; cormorants and herons choked to death on fish, and an eider duck on a toad. There is an almost Poe-like fascination with ghoulishness in accounts of the premature burial of a puffin, smothered while excavating its burrow; a kamikaze diving gannet breaking its neck on the deck of a fishing boat; and the weird behaviour of coveys of partridge flying out to sea, alighting on the waves and drowning *en masse*.

Cherry Kearton's excursions into Africa, ostensibly to record what is there without the perception of human intervention, were in reality very much to do with taming the wilderness; his position as, in Ada Kearton's description, "the first man in the world to shoot with a camera rather than a rifle"[21] inevitably somewhat compromised. His first safaris were treks of days and weeks, the relatively modest retinue of eighteen men fed on food collected in the bush, typically zebra and buck meat. He shot for the pot; also apparently for sport, as James L. Clark's diary for 15 August 1909, reveals: "Kearton went out to shoot fox again in the evening. Later he came in with three spring hares".[22]

Some of the shooting was for protection, from for example a python seen in a tree near the camp on 26 September 1909 although it is not always clear how great the threat would have been had the targets been left alone: "Tuesday, September 28th. About eleven o'clock Kearton said a jackal came to drink and when I looked I saw it was a leopard. Kearton took aim and pulled, but the cartridge missed fire and before I could get a shot, it bolted".

Cherry Kearton took as souvenirs zebra skins, and the head of a rhino shot by James L. Clark. He helped his companions, Clark and William Coates, secure specimens for their collections: "Monday, September 14th. We found lots of game there but no water and on the way back Kearton shot a fine wart hog which he gave to me". He was not always candid about his involvement in this: for example, in *Wild Life Across the World* he notes that on 20 August 1909, "Clark shot a male bush-buck for food", while Clark's diaries for the same date take a different perspective: "I saw two bushbuck feeding some 400 yards from camp on the hill. I stalked and shot the male and when I returned I found the doe which K. had shot from camp at 200 yards, hitting it in the neck. I saved the two specimens #120, #121 for mounting".

Kearton was shadowing the Roosevelt safari, which as we have seen was controversially trigger-happy. His own party was always very much more restrained, but some incidents leave a bad taste: "September 8th. On the way back [Kearton] saw a colobus up a tree and as I had gone off on the side to shoot a dik-dak he called to me to come. We drove it around and he managed to get 5 ft. of film of it. Its jumps from limb to limb were marvelous and it would drop sometimes 20 or 30 ft. to a lower branch. After the picture was taken we drove it from over the river and I shot it".

The urge to tame, at least as far as big game was concerned, reached its apotheosis in 1910 when Kearton returned to Africa with a commission to film the lassoing safari of Charles 'Buffalo' Jones. Another from the roster of muscular adventurers in east Africa in those years, Jones was an American cattle breeder and conservationist ("The Preserver of the American Bison") who, in 1902, had been personally appointed by President Roosevelt as first game warden of Yellowstone National Park. He was later the inspiration for Zane Grey's *The Last of the Plainsmen*. Before the 1910 safari, it was reported that he had roped and tied, often single-handed, "all kinds of wild animals in North America, including the musk-ox, buffalo, grizzly bear, and cougar", and that "his experience with these has led him to believe implicitly that man is the master of all wild beasts".[23] Jones hired two cowboys, Ambrose Means and Marshall Loveless; a guide, the colonialist white hunter Ray Ulyate, who had been Roosevelt's wagon driver; as well as Kearton and assistant cameraman D. W. (Dave) Gobbett. Once assistant manager of the Alhambra Music Hall in Brighton, Gobbett arrived in Africa unable to ride a horse; he was described rather fruitily in the trade press as "well-known to habitués of Cecil Court, several white hunters and a large number of native 'boys'".[24] The Jones safari, a search for an alternative to big

Right: *"Lassoing a rhinoceros"*.

game hunting which Jones believed had already had its day, was a unique attempt to bring the rodeo to east Africa, as a "sporting proposition" to verify whether the methods by which cowboys had won the west could tame the wild nature of another continent.

Kearton, fresh from the Roosevelt safari, was recruited as "an experienced cinematograph photographer and a naturalist of no small reputation".[25] There was at that time no one with his experience of filming in Africa, of "the climatic conditions there—the heat radiation and the different intensities of light", and it seems unlikely that the expedition would have gone ahead without his expertise. To his credit, Kearton was sceptical, questioning "the feasibility of the experiment in the light of what he knew of the African beasts" when interviewed in London by Jones and his field manager, Guy H. Scull, who discerned that "evidently his mind was divided by the dictates of common sense and the sporting instinct". Finally persuaded, Kearton conceded "Well, there's a picture in it, anyway", and signed the papers.

To get seven Europeans into the Rift Valley with their essential kit of lassoes, horses, dogs, cameras, tripods, film and chemicals, took four bullock-wagons, two cooks, five camera boys, seven personal boys, a Masai spearman, and an army of eighty-odd carriers, each with a sixty-pound load, variously components of tents, folding chairs and tables, tinned and bagged food, cooking gear and ammunition. The "mighty company" assembled at Nairobi railway station, the baggage "in stacks, great piles of it... it seemed so utterly out of proportion".[26] It took over four hours to get the complement loaded onto a hired train bound for Kijabe, where the safari proper—a trek in single file, "often to the accompaniment of a monotonous sort of native chant"—began. The direction taken, towards the Sotik Plain, was determined simply by it being "reported to be more or less free from ticks", and therefore favourable for the health of the horses.

The plan of attack was established on the first day, when Ulyate spotted three warthogs in the distance. Kearton and Gobbett set up their cameras, while the cowboys rode off, separated the largest boar from the group, and drove him "snout down, tail in the air, his great tusks showing viciously"[27] to the critical point in front of the camera, where the lasso was swung and the creature brought down in a cloud of dust. From Kearton's point of view it was not a great success, as the horsemen had "driven his quarry straight on to the lens instead of three-quarters on to me". The only usable film was

Left: "Wild dog".

of the animal on the ground, before it was let go and "walked away slowly and disdainfully".[28]

The lesson in framing the shot learned, the expedition succeeded in roping hartebeest, cheetah, eland and zebra, before turning their attentions to bigger beasts. The neck of the giraffe was made for the lariat, the only problem being in retrieving the rope afterwards, when the rather fragile beast would have to be gently brought down with a second rope round the legs to bring the noose within arm's reach. A rhinoceros was cornered and tired over thirty minutes, by inducing it to make repeated charges, before a first rope held. But this was far from sufficient; for over four and a half hours the rhino was harried and numerous lines broken before, half worn out, the creature was made fast to a tree. The ultimate prize, a lion, turned out to be something of an anti-climax. A female was run to ground in a thicket; a lasso that tangled in some overhanging scrub was prodded down with a stick, and the creature provoked into charging into the noose. The only animal not released into the wild, the lioness was caged and sent to Bronx Park Zoological Gardens in New York, where it lived until 1921.

It had been less than a year since Kearton had assembled oddments of footage of African townscapes and landscapes, inhabitants and wildlife, with an American ex-president blazing his trail of glory through it all, into a scrapbook of a film. But the Kearton-Jones safari represented an entirely different attitude to cinema. Film was no longer the souvenir, but the *raison d'être* of the expedition. Instead of a documentary of impressions, there was a manufactured story which the film shaped itself to. And somehow, along the way, the Keartons' early credo of portraying nature unaffected was left in the scrub; the film had nothing to do with animal behaviour. The cowboys might as well have been lassoing steam trains or orchestras. It was all to do with conquest, with advancing the philosophy subscribed to by Buffalo Jones and by Cherry Kearton, of man the invincible. It was an entirely artificial vehicle for celluloid heroism.

The stories Ada typed up in 1925 led to a series of children's books inspired by the Kearton menagerie. This included a number of legitimately acquired animals—chimps, a mongoose, grey monkey, snakes, a "giant spider", etc.—brought home as pets from Cherry's travels, established in the early 1920s at first at St John's Wood; when this became unmanageable, in the more extensive grounds of the house at Great Ivy Mill, Tovil. Cherry and Ada were immensely fond of their pets, whose place in the household was spelled out in such book titles

Above: *"Mary sat smoking her cigarette".*

as *My Happy Family* and *My Animal Friendships*. They took particular pleasure in behaviour that suggested ('aped') that of humans, most particularly children. One consequence of the years spent living in close company was that Cherry, in his books, films and lectures, grew to emphasize a human interpretation of individual and social animal activity. This was compounded by deliberately making little people of the chimps, by dressing them up in children's clothes, taking them on trips to the seaside, letting them smoke pipes and having them drink tea at the table, inspiration for the London Zoo tea parties. (There were of course many other examples across the twentieth century of experiments, whose greater or lesser pretence at scientific endeavour was often compromised by attachment, with "enculturated" apes raised in a human cultural setting and "encouraged to adopt many

Above: *Cherry Kearton with "nature's little comedians".*

of the aspects of human experience, including daily activities, use of human toys and tools, world view, communication, and sometimes manners and clothing".[29] Scientifically, there appears little evidence that any of the observed behaviours demonstrated learning rather than mimicry).

In 1929, Cherry and Ada laid plans for a new adventure, a three-month sojourn on Dassen Island, an outcrop in the Atlantic lying about 35 miles north of Cape Town. Cherry had visited here before, in 1921, in weather conditions so extreme that four consecutive nights were spent in rough seas attempting landfall. Kearton seems to have made little more than a cursory inspection of the island before returning to the boat "... and so I got away from Penguin Island, which I shall never see again. Nothing would induce me to revisit the place, especially in stormy weather".[30] But induced he was; they would be the only human inhabitants, staying in a warden's shack and sharing the island with hundreds of thousands (five million, in Kearton's estimate) of black-footed penguins. The material they gathered would spawn a full-length book, a lecture tour, and a feature film for which a new production company, Cherry Kearton Films, was founded.

The penguins became, of course, the Keartons' new animal family and friends. There may have been no dressing up, pipe smoking or tea parties, but the anthropomorphism which had been nurtured during the Great Ivy Mill days found its perfect expression in the comic capers of "nature's little comedians", as the subtitle of the Dassen film dubbed them. In a way, the penguins proved the ideal subject for Kearton's redacted nature-view: cute yet exotic, endlessly photogenic, amusing, cartoon-like parodies of themselves. The book, *The Island of Penguins*, introduced "The Magistrate", "The Tramp", "The Cherub", "Charlie Chaplin", penguins "proud and... meek, the bully, the mischief maker, the comfortable old gentleman, the despised weakling and the social outcast". The penguins were likened to "old gentlemen, young men about town, youthful mothers, sedate matrons. But more than anything they are like..."—how better to suggest diminished humans?— "children".[31]

The book followed the seasons of a pair of black-foots, dubbed "Mr and Mrs Penguin" (in the film *Dassen*, we meet "Frank and Flora Flatfeet"). A deal of accurate observation was mixed, in an archly condescending commentary, with a human interpretation of social life. These included "walking out" and "engagement", leading to "the marriage ceremony" and subsequent creation of a "beautiful new house" with a "charming bedroom" furnished with "elegant furniture" and a "beautiful carpet", maintained by "Mrs Penguin's... very busy housekeeping".[32] These analogies for human domestic, even suburban, conventions, were reinforced by a degree of misinterpretation through misunderstanding, for example of parent penguins "teaching" their offspring to swim.[33] Further distortion arose through the reduction to entertainment, though this would become, and remain, something of a given; take for example a comment of Alastair Fothergill, executive producer of David Attenborough's *Frozen Planet*: "...in the south, the stars are the penguins. We knew we could get lots of funny shots of them".[34]

In his comprehensive survey of the genre, *Wildlife Films*, Derek Bousé suggests that "*Dassan* [sic] betrayed how little Kearton had learned about the penguins themselves, their pair-bonding behaviour, and the subtle complexities of their social existence".[35] The defence which Kearton offered in *Adventures with Animals and Men*, if strangely oblique, revealed a commercial rationale: "But since it was now clear that a film that has an element of fiction in it was meat for adults whereas one that contained nothing but the truth could only be exhibited mainly to children, I determined to include stories in my films—and yet to avoid departing from my principles. My films should show stories, but the setting of them should be truth. These stories should be the vehicles to carry studies of real natural history...".[36]

Whether or not that made Cherry Kearton a "fableist and nature faker of the highest order" as Bousé has alleged,[37] it certainly muddied the water. What Kearton appears to have meant by "stories" are narratives of human rituals and customs overlaid onto depictions of the social interactions of animals, in this case penguins. In both book and film, objective observation is so thoroughly mixed with skewed interpretation that we can no longer sieve "truth" from "stories". As to what he meant by "real natural history", this seems to be interchangeable with the evidence shown on screen: we know that it is "real nature" because it is also, in Greg Mitman's coinage, "reel nature".

The fact is that Cherry Kearton was less zoologist than nature-lover, less educator than crusader. It is true that the dominant voice—populist, entertaining, simplistic, parochial—is one he adopted seemingly as the lowest common denominator for the largest audience, and one which at times came close to adopting him. It is debatable, of course, whether the merit of attracting greater public interest in wildlife through films such as this is balanced by the missed opportunity of educating and informing, even of a smaller audience, through commentaries incorporating accurate observation and research, rather than slapstick and punchlines. One side of the argument is made by Derek Bousé, who found *Dassen* "one of the most spectacular missed opportunities to steer the wildlife genre toward accurate portrayals of the family and social lives of animals".[38] But Kearton's intention was not to produce a film "made by scientists for scientists [and] seen by few but scientists".[39] In promoting an alternative to the by-then ubiquitous big-game and hunting features, he attracted his largest audience ever; the book was a best-seller translated into several languages. Had it been a straight documentary, (e.g. *The Social Life of the Black-footed Penguin*) a select few may have learned a little. As it was, a cinema audience almost as numerous as the Dassen penguin population was entertained, stimulated and, in more than one notable example, provoked into pursuing for themselves a fuller picture of "real natural history".

Right: *Black-footed penguins, Dassen Island.*

One reason Cherry and Ada Kearton's venture with the penguins on Dassen Island has been singled out for particular criticism is that it most resembles the modern approach—to film a single species, and the varied aspects of its behaviour, over a long period of time. Not surprisingly, its perceived failure to meet attendant modern standards has led to it—and in its wake some other work by the Keartons—being judged rather detrimentally. Better, and fairer, to consider instead how much Richard and Cherry Kearton contributed to the setting of those standards. Naturalists, as suggested in the Introduction, are sometimes irked to find them wed more to the image and the story than to the rigours of science; but the stream of spectacularly successful modern television series depicting the natural world, which have the esteem of the scientific community, follow the Keartons' principles to the letter.

Equally, there is less distance between the practices of the Keartons and contemporary photographers than might appear. Technological advances such as high-speed cameras, powerful optical zoom lenses, and rapid-fire shutters, together with the vivacity of modern colour, enable images way beyond the capabilities of the Keartons and their cameras. But the contemporary quest is the same as theirs, for 'how and wow' photographs: those that illustrate 'how' animal behaviours and physiological mechanisms operate, and those that extend the range of human vision to capture beautiful, insightful and sensational moments, provoking the collective 'wow'.

Since the Keartons, so much about nature has been learned, and so many millions of photographs taken, that no serious nature photographer would take on projects so general in their nature as those that absorbed the Keartons—to photograph all the breeding birds, or their nests, or eggs, in Britain, or to take the first ever film of mammals on distant continents. Those goals have been achieved for us, by the Keartons and by their contemporaries. But the greater legacy of both brothers, as I hope this book has demonstrated, is a body of work that bears repeated viewing, pictures that speak for themselves and promote the tenet succinctly proposed by Richard Kearton: "Teaching through the eye".

Left: *Giraffe.*

Notes

Abbreviations

AAM	*Adventures with Animals and Men* (CK)
ACD	*The Animals Came to Drink* (CK)
ACR	*The Adventures of Cock Robin and His Mate* (RK)
AHWN	*At Home with Wild Nature* (RK)
AJR	*The Adventures of Jack Rabbit* (RK)
ANP	*A Naturalist's Pilgrimage* (RK)
BBH	*Baby Birds at Home* (RK)
BBN	*British Birds' Nests* (RK)
BNE	*Birds' Nests, Eggs, and Egg Collecting* (RK)
CKA	*The Cherry Kearton Animal Book* (CK)
CKT	*Cherry Kearton's Travels* (CK)
FLT	*The Fairyland of Living Things* (RK)
ILL	*In the Land of the Lion* (CK)
IOP	*The Island of Penguins* (CK)
IVA	*I Visit the Antipodes* (CK)
KNP	*Keartons' Nature Pictures* (RK)
MAF	*My Animal Friendships* (CK)
MDS	*My Dog Simba* (CK)
MFT	*My Friend Toto* (CK)
MHA	*My Happy Animals* (CK)
MHC	*My Happy Chimpanzee* (CK)
MHF	*My Happy Family* (CK)
MWH	*My Woodland Home* (CK)
NCS	*Nature's Carol Singers* (RK)
NHS	*The Natural History of Selborne* (RK)
OBF	*Our Bird Friends* (RK)
ORBB	*Our Rarer British Breeding Birds* (RK)
OS	*On Safari* (Ada Kearton)
PBB	*The Pocket Book of British Birds* (RK)
PFN	*Pictures from Nature* (RK)
PI	*Penguin Island* (CK)
PWLW	*Photographing Wild Life across the World* (CK)
RKND	*Richard Kearton Nature Diaries*
SADB	*Strange Adventures in Dicky Bird Land* (RK)
SSA	*Shifting Sands of Algeria* (CK)
TCA	*Through Central Africa from East to West* (CK)
TLR	*The Lion's Roar* (CK)
WBA	*Wild Bird Adventures* (RK)
WLAH	*Wild Life at Home* (RK)
WLAW	*Wild Life Across the World* (CK)
WNC	*With Nature and a Camera* (RK)
WNW	*Wild Nature's Ways* (RK)
WWN	*Wonders of Wild Nature* (RK)

Introduction

1 Hosking & Lowes, p.18.
2 PI, p.9.
3 www.pbs.org/wnet/nature/attenboroughs-life-stories-preview/8146/
4 ANP, pp.112–113.
5 Simon Baker, discussing the exhibition he curated for Tate Modern, 'Performing for the Camera', quoted in Sean O'Hagan, 'Caught in the Act', *Guardian*, 1 February 2016.
6 *Attenborough: 60 Years in the Wild.* Episode 1: Life on Camera. BBC, 2012.
7 Obituary, *Guardian*, 18 February 2003.

1. At home with the Keartons

1 AHWN, p.90.
2 OBF, p.viii.
3 ANP, p.28.
4 ANP, p.76.
5 ANP, p.81.
6 ANP, p.88.
7 ANP, p.82.
8 ANP, p.9.
9 ANP, p.9.
10 Letters to the author.
11 *Dundee Evening Post*, 22 January 1904.
12 Cherry Kearton II, 1967, pp.19–20.
13 AAM, p.64.
14 AAM, p.75.
15 AAM, p.102.
16 AAM, p.201.
17 www.frontiersmenhistorian.info/intro.htm
18 AAM, p.204.
19 www.frontiersmen.org.au/kearton.htm
20 AAM, pp.209–210.
21 OS, p.50.
22 Reported widely, see for example *Lancashire Evening Post*, 19 April 1920.
23 OS, p.43.

2. The first nature photography book

1 ANP, p.110.
2 Piersssene, 1964.
3 Carwardine, 2012.
4 'The camera among the seabirds'. *Strand Magazine*, Vol. 4, 1892, pp.471–474.

5 Carwardine, 2012.
6 Hosking & Lowes, p.11.
7 Brower, p.110.
8 ANP, p.104.
9 ANP, p.109.
10 AAM, pp.5–6.
11 MWH, p.18.
12 AAM, p.6.
13 ANP, p.110.
14 WLAH, pp.2–4.
15 Hosking, 1970, p.279.
16 See for example BBN, p.xiii.
17 Pearson's, 1900, p.466.
18 WNC, pp.vii–viii.
19 OBF, pp.32–91.
20 Brower, p.117.
21 Beaton, p.24.

3. The Kearton partnership

1 RKND, 25 June 1908.
2 WLAW, p.xvi.
3 ANP, p.9.
4 MWH, p.79.
5 WLAW, pp.xxvi–xxvii.
6 MHF, p.9.
7 IVA, p.32.
8 IVA, p.18.
9 MWH, p.19.
10 Quoted in W. R. Mitchell, 2000, p.130.
11 FLT, preface.
12 KNP, Vol. I, p.iii.
13 RKND, 7 June 1900.
14 RKND, 10 June 1913.
15 WNW, p.89.
16 WNW, p.10.
17 WNW, pp.88–90.
18 BBN, p.x.
19 Pearson's, 1900, p.470.
20 Pearson's, 1900, p.470.
21 Quoted in Ellison, 1945.
22 RKND, 14 May 1919.
23 RKND, 5 May 1905.
24 RKND, 6 May 1904.
25 WLAH, p.151.
26 WLAH, p.143.
27 OBF, pp.86, 88–89.
28 OBF, pp.98–100.
29 FLT, pp.143–145.
30 OBF, p.169.
31 AHWN, p.3.
32 OBF, p.169.
33 OBF, p.195.
34 Robert Browning, 'Home Thoughts from Abroad', 1845.
35 OBF, p.180.
36 WNC, pp.90–92.
37 SADB, pp.viii–ix.
38 See Chapter 1, p.32
39 www.mocavo.co.uk/Bulletin-of-the-British-Ornithologists-Club-Volume-21-23-1907-09-Volume-volume-21-23-1907-09/383637/102
40 Bryony Dixon, www.screenonline.org.uk/film/id/1354742/

4. The stuffed ox and other hides

1 PBB, p.2.
2 AAM, p.29.
3 WNW, pp.1–2.
4 NHS, p.13.
5 WNW, p.46.
6 WLAH, pp.10–11.
7 Morris, 2003.
8 WNW, pp.2–3.
9 Cherry Kearton II, 1967, p.16.
10 WNW, p.6.
11 AAM, p.9.
12 WNW, pp.6–7.
13 WNW, p.1.
14 WNW, p.4.
15 AAM, p.50.
16 WNW, p.12.
17 WNW, pp.8–10.
18 WNW, pp.13–20.
19 WNW, pp.32–36.
20 WNW, pp.21–31.
21 WNW, pp.37–41.
22 WNW, pp.244–257.
23 WNW, pp.100–103.
24 MWH, p.155.
25 AAM, pp.44–45.
26 AAM, pp.48–49.

5. The man who shot Roosevelt…

1 AAM, p.66.
2 www.pbs.org/nationalparks/people/historical/roosevelt/
3 See Richard E. Grant: The History of Safari, BBC Television, 2012; Cameron, 1990, pp.15–37.
4 Roosevelt, Camera Shots at Big Game.
5 Mitman, p.11.
6 AAM, p.66.
7 AAM, p.43.
8 AAM, p.46.
9 Gouyon, pp.27, 31, 32–35.
10 O'Toole, p.72.
11 O'Toole, p.67.
12 See O'Toole, pp.59, 65, 69.
13 WLAW, p.90.
14 AAM, pp.66–67.
15 AAM, p.68.
16 Unger, p.103.
17 Hasegawa, 2010.
18 WLAW, pp.100–101.
19 WLAW, p.101.
20 Moving Picture World, 10 September 1910.
21 Various clips and edits were circulated, a shorter version being titled With Roosevelt in Africa. The Library of Congress hosts a 13-minute cut on YouTube.
22 Variety, April 1910.

23 Gunning, p.63.
24 Tobias, pp.83–102.
25 WLAW, pp.v–vi.
26 www.mnh.si.edu/onehundredyears/
expeditions/SI-Roosevelt_Expedition.html
27 Barnouw, Eric. *Documentary: A History of
the Non-fiction Film*. New York: OUP, 1993.
28 AAM, pp.279–289.
29 Cameron, 1994, pp.50–51.

6. Deceiving wild creatures

1 OS, p.159.
2 FLT, p.48.
3 PWLW, publisher's note.
4 WLAW, p.225.
5 Jackson's widowbird.
6 WLAW, p.221.
7 PWLW, p.198.
8 WLAW, p.13.
9 PWLW, p.201.
10 PWLW, p.202.
11 PWLW, p.203.
12 MWH, p.20.
13 WLAW, p.221.
14 PWLW, p.199.
15 WLAW, p.236.
16 WLAW, p.221.
17 PWLW, p.200.
18 OS, pp.65–66.
19 OS, p.49.
20 AAM, pp.20–41.
21 *Cambridge Independent Press*, 8 May 1908.
22 *Sevenoaks Chronicle*, 8 May 1908.
23 *London Daily News*, 2 May 1908.
24 *Daily Chronicle*; reprinted in *North Otago
Times*, 5 August 1908.
25 OS, pp.47–49.
26 WLAW, p.43.
27 FLT, pp.6–7; MWH, p.57; FLT pp.48–50;
MWH, p.78.
28 MWH, p.38.
29 James L. Clark, Diaries.
30 Barry Paine, obituary of Eric Ashby,
Guardian, 18 February 2003.
31 WLAW, p.238.
32 WLAW, p.240.
33 PWLW, p.210.
34 WLAW, p.224.
35 WLAW, pp.225–241.
36 PWLW, p.210.

7. The wildness of wild life

1 Henry David Thoreau, *Walden: Or, Life in
the Woods*.
2 WNC, p.336.
3 WLAH, p.ix.
4 WLAH, p.viii.
5 See Chapter 6, p.141–142
6 See Springer, 2011.
7 BBN, p.xii.

8 AHWN, p.vi.
9 ORBB, p.ix.
10 ORBB, pp.ix–x.
11 ORBB, pp.xiii–xiv.
12 ORBB, pp.vii, xi.
13 Cherry Kearton II, 1967, p.17.
14 BBAH, p.2.
15 RKND, 20 May 1920.
16 WNC, Chapters 2–5 & 8–10.
17 WNC, pp.295–310.
18 WLAW, p.167.
19 WNW, pp.47–48.
20 RKND, 27 May 1907.
21 OS, p.49.
22 James L. Clark, Diaries.
23 Scull, 1911.
24 *The Bioscope*, 30 June 1910.
25 Scull, 1911.
26 WLAW, p.164.
27 WLAW, p.168.
28 PWLW, p.147.
29 H. Lyn Miles, 'Anthropomorphism, Apes
and Language', in Mitchell, Thompson &
Miles, 1997.
30 PWLW, p.247.
31 IOP, p.221.
32 IOP, pp.58–65.
33 IOP, pp.142–143.
34 'How we made... *Frozen Planet*', *Guardian*,
20 October 2015.
35 Bousé, p.171.
36 AAM, p.279.
37 Bousé, p.113.
38 Bousé, p.171.
39 Bousé, p.155.

Richard & Cherry Kearton: Bibliography and filmography

Books by Richard Kearton

Birds' Nests, Eggs, and Egg Collecting
With illustrations by Alexander Francis Lydon. Cloth, 96pp. London: Cassell, 1890. New and enlarged edition, 1896.
The enlarged edition details 252 species, including "all British-breeding birds that now have any reasonable claim for treatment", and "a number of more or less familiar winter visitors that do not stay to breed with us".

British Birds' Nests: How, Where and When to Find and Identify Them
With photographs by Cherry Kearton. Introduction by R. Bowdler Sharpe, LL.D. Cloth, 384pp. London: Cassell, 1895.
Text arranged under species in alphabetical order gives details for each of: description of parent birds; situation and locality; materials; eggs; time; remarks including residency, song notes and description, local and other names.

With Nature and a Camera: Being the Adventures and Observations of a Field Naturalist and an Animal Photographer
With photographs by Cherry Kearton. Cloth, 368pp. London: Cassell, 1897.
Chapters on St Kilda; gamekeepers; nests, eggs and young; where birds sleep; sea birds and their haunts; bird catchers and duck decoying; methods of photography.

Wild Life at Home: How to Study and Photograph it
With photographs by Cherry Kearton. Cloth, 188pp. London: Cassell, 1898. New and revised edition, 204pp, 1907.
Described in preface as "…such a manual as will, we honestly believe, enable every one of average intelligence and perseverance to go out into the fields with a camera and secure pictures equal to anything we have ourselves obtained…"

Our Rarer British Breeding Birds: Their Nests, Eggs and Summer Haunts
With photographs by Cherry Kearton. Cloth, 156pp. London: Cassell, 1899.
Field guide, alphabetical by species, with description of bird, breeding grounds, nest and eggs, etc., with RK's observations and anecdotes, "to be regarded as a supplement to our former work on British Birds' Nests…"

Our Bird Friends: A Book for All Boys and Girls
With photographs by Cherry Kearton. Cloth, 216pp. London: Cassell, 1900. New and revised edition, 1923.
For "young readers… a chatty though accurate little volume dealing with just such phases of bird life are likely to attract attention…" including feeding, nests and eggs, young, feathers and flight, calls and song notes.

Strange Adventures in Dicky Bird Land
With photographs by Cherry Kearton. Cloth, 195pp. London: Cassell, 1901.
Illustrated children's book of "stories told by mother birds to amuse their chicks, and overheard by Richard Kearton FZS".

The Natural History of Selborne
Gilbert White, with photographs by Cherry & Richard Kearton. Cloth, 294pp. London: Cassell, 1902. Second edition, cloth, 248pp. London: Arrowsmith, 1924.
A selection from Selborne illustrated with photographs taken on location.

Wild Nature's Ways
With photographs by Cherry & Richard Kearton. Cloth, 296pp. London: Cassell, 1903.
Chapters on birds and their habitats, birds in winter, "some curiosities of wild life" and methods of photography.

Left: *"Young Kestrel"*.

The Adventures of Cock Robin and His Mate
With photographs by Cherry & Richard Kearton. Cloth, 240pp. London: Cassell, 1904.
Illustrated children's story book.

Pictures from Nature
With photographs by Cherry & Richard Kearton. Limited edition of 100 copies in cloth portfolio; popular edition in paper folder. London: Cassell, 1905.
Fifteen choice Rembrandt photogravures of birds and animals photographed in their natural surroundings, in a "sumptuous portfolio".

Nature's Carol Singers
With photographs by Cherry & Richard Kearton. Cloth, 256pp. London: Cassell, 1906.
A guide for the novice birdwatcher to "appearance, haunts, habits, nests, eggs songs and call notes of the winged melodists that breed in the various parts of the British Isles", describing 45 species.

The Fairyland of Living Things
With photographs by Cherry & Richard Kearton. Cloth, 182pp. London: Cassell, 1907.
"In this little book I have tried by word and picture to give children a peep into the wonderful fairy-land of the living things of the countryside." A natural history primer for children and young adults, covering British birds, mammals, reptiles, plants and insects.

British Birds' Nests
With photographs by Cherry Kearton. New edition revised and enlarged. Cloth, 520pp. London: Cassell, 1907.
The revised edition superseded both British Birds' Nests *and* Our Rarer British Breeding Birds. *It includes revisions of the texts and the "best of the pictures" from both volumes, "together with all the appropriate photographs secured during the last seven years".*

Keartons' Nature Pictures
With photographs by Cherry & Richard Kearton. Cloth, 2 vols., 96pp each plus plates. London: Cassell, 1910.
Coffee-table size volumes with full-size plates "beautifully reproduced in photogravure, colour and black and white" and descriptions arranged by species.

The Adventures of Jack Rabbit
With photographs by Richard & Grace Kearton. Cloth, 248pp. London: Cassell, 1911.
Children's book in the style of Strange Adventures in Dicky Bird Land, *"an intimate study of the perils and adventures that beset the lives of wild rabbits…"*

Baby Birds at Home
With photographs by Richard & Grace Kearton. Cloth, 128pp. London: Cassell, 1912.
A children's guide to nests, eggs and fledglings of 64 common species, "prepared in order to give boys and girls who love the countryside… a little gallery of faithful pictures of baby birds amidst their natural surroundings, and secondly, a short and simple account of the interesting habits of their parents".

Wonders of Wild Nature
With photographs by Richard & Grace Kearton. Cloth, 176pp. London: Cassell, 1915.
"An account of my wanderings in search of sun pictures and fresh observations during the last three years", in and around London, the Shetlands, Outer Hebrides, Saltee Islands, the polders and meers of Holland, and on Norwegian mountains.

At Home with Wild Nature
With photographs by Cherry & Richard Kearton. Cloth, 164pp. London: Cassell, 1922.
Anecdotes, curiosities, accidents and superstitions relating to wild birds, with photographs mostly of nesting birds.

Wild Bird Adventures: A Nature Story Book for Boys and Girls
With photographs by Richard Kearton. Cloth, 184pp. London: Cassell, 1923.
More mature children's tales of birdlife taken from real events in 27 chapters, each a short story about a particular species, including descriptions of locations around Caterham Valley and the Dales, methods of photography, etc.

The Pocket Book of British Birds
By Richard Kearton FZS and Howard Bentham. With photographs by Cherry, Richard & John Kearton. Cloth, 390pp. London: Cassell, 1925.
A field guide describing a total of 265 species, and believed to contain "the most complete collection of photographs of British birds ever brought within the covers of a small volume".

A Naturalist's Pilgrimage
With photographs by Cherry & Richard Kearton. Cloth, 246pp. London: Cassell, 1926.
Autobiography, reminiscences and anecdotes in three books, dealing respectively with ancestors, Dales and Fells, and the years 1862–82; Cassell, writing, photography and natural history, and the years 1882–97; lecturing and travelling, and the years 1897–1926.

Above: *"Fox cub: lying with his head out of the 'earth'".*

Books by Cherry Kearton

Wild Life Across the World
Introduction by Theodore Roosevelt.
Foreword by Richard Kearton. Cloth, 286pp.
London: Hodder & Stoughton, 1913.

Through Central Africa from East to West
Written by James Barnes. Cloth, 284pp.
London: Cassell, 1915.

Photographing Wild Life Across the World
Cloth, 320pp. London: Arrowsmith, 1923.
"Contains about two-thirds of [Wild Life Across the World], *rewritten and carefully edited, together with new records... Of the illustrations in the earlier volume eleven are retained, and to them are added seventy-three which have not hitherto appeared in any volume".*

Shifting Sands of Algeria
Cloth, 306pp. London: Arrowsmith, 1924.

My Friend Toto
Cloth, 128pp. London: Arrowsmith,
September 1925. (My Library of Animal
Friends, Vol.I).
The Adventures of a Chimpanzee and the Story of his Journey from the Congo to London.

My Dog Simba
Cloth, 128pp. London: Arrowsmith,
September 1926. (My Library of Animal
Friends, Vol.II).
The Adventures of a Fox-terrier who Fought a Lion in Africa.

My Happy Family
Cloth, 128pp. London: Arrowsmith, 1927.
(My Library of Animal Friends, Vol.III).
The Adventures of Mary the Chimpanzee and The Story of her Friendship with a Fox-Terrier and a Mongoose.

My Happy Chimpanzee
Cloth, 128pp. London: Arrowsmith, 1927.
(My Library of Animal Friends, Vol.V).
The Adventures of Mary, the Wonderful Chimpanzee, at the Seaside.

My Animal Friendships
Cloth, 128pp. London: Arrowsmith, 1928.
(My Library of Animal Friends, Vol.VIII).
The Adventures of Timmy the Rat, Chuey the Cheetah, Robin Parker the Mongoose, Mr. Penguin, Jane the Elephant, and Mrs. Spider.

Above: "Young wheatears".

My Happy Animals
Cloth, 256pp. London: Arrowsmith, April 1929. (The Kearton Readers: II).
The Story of Mary the Chimpanzee, Robin the Mongoose and Tommy the Terrier, and their adventures with their friend Peter Turner. 'My Happy Family' and 'My Happy Chimpanzee' bound together in one volume.

In the Land of the Lion
Cloth, 256pp. London: Arrowsmith, 1929.
"The majority of the illustrations in this book were taken on one of my most recent expeditions to Central Africa, and are part of a cinematograph film produced by me for Cherry Kearton Films Ltd."

The Island of Penguins
Cloth, 222pp. London: Longmans, 1930. US edition New York: McBride & Co. 1931.
Dedicated "To the memory of Dick, my dear brother and comrade over many rough roads".

The Animals Came to Drink
Cloth, 88pp. London: Longmans, 1932.

The Lion's Roar (A tale)
Cloth, 188pp. London: Longmans, 1934.

Adventures with Animals and Men
Cloth, 292pp. London: Longmans, 1935.
Autobiography

I Visit the Antipodes
Cloth, 232pp. London: Jarrolds, 1937.

My Woodland Home
Cloth, 156pp. London: Jarrolds, 1938.

Cherry Kearton's Travels
Cloth, 286pp. London: Robert Hale, 1941.

The Cherry Kearton Animal Book
Cloth, 168pp. London: Hutchinson, 1958.
The bulk of the pet books, collected and revised, including Simba the Lion Dog (from My Dog Simba*), Toto (from* My Friend Toto*), Animal Friendships (from* My Animal Friendships*), and Mary (from* My Happy Chimpanzee*). Copyright and introduction by Ada Cherry Kearton.*

Penguin Island
Cloth, 112pp. London: Hutchinson, 1960.
Includes much of The Island of Penguins*, with some new material. Foreword by Peter Scott. Copyright Ada Cherry Kearton.*

Films by Cherry Kearton

Sea Bird Colonies
Richard and Cherry Kearton. 800ft, B&W, silent. Urban Trading Company, Autumn 1907.
Birds on the Farne Islands and Bass Rock.

Our Insect Summer Visitors
Richard and Cherry Kearton. 430ft, B&W, silent. Urban Trading Company, 1907.

Reptiles and their greedy ways
Richard and Cherry Kearton. 450ft, B&W, silent. Urban Trading Company, 1907.

Wild Birds at Home
Richard and Cherry Kearton. 850ft, B&W, silent. Urban Trading Company, catalogue, 1908.

Wild Birds: Old and Young
Richard and Cherry Kearton. B&W, silent. Urban Trading Company, catalogue, 1908.

Haunts of Wild Birds
Richard and Cherry Kearton. 1030ft, B&W, silent. Urban Trading Company, catalogue, August 1909.

Scenes in Massua
Cherry Kearton. About 5 mins, B&W, silent. Warwick Trading Company, 1910.

With Roosevelt in Africa
Cherry Kearton. 900ft (about 10 mins), B&W, silent. Warwick Trading Company, April 1910.
Also listed as Roosevelt in Africa, *2000ft.*

Lion Spearing
Cherry Kearton. 450ft, B&W, silent. Warwick Trading Company, 1910.
Also titled Native Lion Fighting *and* Native Lion Hunt.

Lassoing Wild Animals in Africa
About 20 mins, B&W, silent. Directed Cherry Kearton. Pathé Frères, 1910.
Record of Kearton-Jones expedition to Kenya, March–April 1910.

A Primitive Man's Career to Civilisation
248 ft. Photography Cherry Kearton. Warwick Trading Company, 1911.
African "savages" learning to shave, wear Western clothes, go to church and read and write.

Reise Nach dem Innern Afrikas
Director Cherry Kearton. About 13 mins, B&W, silent. Warwick Trading Company, 1911.
Apparently a compilation of Scenes in Massua, *the start and end of* Lassoing Wild Animals, *and some of* Roosevelt in Africa.

With the Greeks in the Firing Line
B&W, silent. GB/France/Germany, 1913.
Footage of the Second Balkan War, including the battle at Salonika.

Across Africa from East to West
Photography Cherry Kearton, edited Corden. B&W, silent. Warwick Trading Company, 1914.
Footage of the Barnes-Kearton safari.

The Shirker's Nightmare
650ft, B&W, silent. Cherry Kearton Limited, 1914.
Patriotic comedy.

Whirlpool of War
Weekly news cinemagazine to accompany Warwick Bioscope Chronicle, 33 titles produced by Cherry Kearton between August 1914 and February 1915.
Titles include: Antwerp under shot and shell (Part 15). About 7 mins, B&W, silent. With the warriors at Ypres (Part 19). About 10 mins, B&W, silent. With the British and French in Flanders (Part 21). About 5 mins, B&W, silent. Fight for the Coast (Part 23). About 5 mins, B&W, silent.

Aerial Invasion Frustrated
Drama, 1,000ft, B&W, silent. Cherry Kearton Limited, March 1915.

Our Boys
Cherry Kearton Limited, 1915.
Adapted stage tragi-comedy by H. J. Byron.

With Our Expeditionary Force in British East Africa
Footage released by Samson Film Company, photography Cherry Kearton, March 1916.

Our Grip on the Huns
Footage released by Samson Film Company, photography Cherry Kearton, August 1916.
Also released as The Cherry Kearton African War Film.

On the Equator
Director Cherry Kearton, editor Frank Green.
About 8 mins, B&W. 1923.
Travelogue of Uganda around the Semliki River.

Wild Life Across the World
Director, photography Cherry Kearton. 1923.
*Includes 'The mystery of the Waterhole',
'Lassoing Big Game in Africa', 'Spearing
Man-Eaters' and 'The Swamps of the Semliki'.*

Toto's Wife
Cherry Kearton Film Company, 1924.

Life in the Sudan
Director of photography Cherry Kearton.
B&W. 1925.

With Cherry Kearton in the Jungle
5 reels, B&W, silent. Director Kearton. Cherry
Kearton Film Company, 1927.

Tembi
Feature. Cherry Kearton Film Company, 1929.

Dassen: An adventure in search of laughter, featuring nature's greatest little comedians
Director Cherry Kearton / Ada Kearton.
Cherry Kearton Film Company, 1930.
Penguins on Dassen Island, S. Africa.

Mototo
Director Cherry Kearton, 1932.
*Feature about a lion cub born in Africa, brought
to England as a pet, and given to the Scottish
Zoological Gardens.*

Sally Sallies Forth
Director Cherry Kearton, 1933.
Also released as Sally's Day Out.

The Big Game of Life
About 70 mins, B&W. British Columbia
Productions, 1935.
*Opens with shots of Muker, concludes with
command performance of films at Windsor
Castle. Features Theodore Roosevelt, John Boyes.
Directed, commentary Kearton; edited James
Anderson.*

Journey to Adventure: A film chronicle of Cherry Kearton
43 mins, B&W. Select Classic Productions,
1947.
*Reconstruction of Kearton's life, with excerpts
from his films. Directed Kearton, produced
Burt Hyams, written and compiled by James
Anderson from Kearton's personal account.*

A Million and One
36 mins, B&W, sound. Select Classic
Productions, 1947.
*Compilation of extracts from Dassen and
Mototo. Directed, scripted and commentary
James Anderson, photography Cherry Kearton.*

African Ambassador: Memoirs of Lady Arabella Ape
Photography Cherry Kearton. Montana Film,
1949.

Man of the Wilds
James M. Anderson. 1954.

Miscellaneous Kearton titles
Including books by other Kearton family members, and titles of especial relevance

Familiar Wild Birds Part 19
By W. Swaysland [series editor] "Contents
of this part: Eggs and Egg Collecting, with
notes on Birds' Eggs by R. Kearton, F.Z.S.,
illustrated by A. Thorburn and others". Edited
from Birds' Nest, Eggs, and Egg-Collecting.
Paper, pages numbered 97–128. London:
Cassell, 9 December 1903.

The Nature-Lover's Handbook
By Richard Kearton, John J. Ward, H. Purefoy
Fitzgerald, Henry Irving and S. C. Bensusan.
Cloth, 268pp. London: Cassell, 1911.

The Birds of the British Isles and their Eggs
By T. A. Coward. Illustrations by Archibald
Thorburn, photographic illustrations by
Richard Kearton and others. London; New
York: F. Warne, 1919.

Bird Life in England
John Kearton
"With 48 illustrations". Cloth, 244pp. London:
Philip Allan, 1931.

Above: *"Stoat about to drag dead rabbit away"*.

Nature Smiling Through
John Kearton and Hugh W. S. Walwyn
Cloth, 256pp. London: Hutchinson, 1934.

Evolution Out of Doors
Henry J. C. Molony
A study of sex differences and animal
coloration. Photos by Cherry and John
Kearton. Cloth, 248pp. London: Hutchinson,
1937.

Under African Skies
Ada Forrest
Cloth, 248pp. London: Robert Hale, 1941.

Nature Memories
John Kearton
Cloth, 152pp. London: Jarrolds, 1950.

On Safari
Ada Kearton
An autobiography. Cloth, 192pp. London:
Robert Hale, 1956.

*Watch the Birdie!: The Life and Times of
Richard and Cherry Kearton, Pioneers
of Wildlife Photography*
W. R. Mitchell
Paper, 144pp. Settle: Castleberg, 2001.

*In the Belly of an Ox: The Unexpected
Photographic Adventures of Richard
and Cherry Kearton*
Rebecca Bond
Cloth, 32pp. Boston: Houghton Mifflin
Harcourt, 2009.
*Children's format picturebook with charming
watercolours derived mostly from original
Kearton photographs.*

"I have frequently been asked which of my thousands and thousands of photographs of wild life I most greatly prize. I have never had any hesitation in answering: 'My picture of a beautiful black-throated diver sitting on her nest built upon a wee island in a Hebridean loch'."—Richard Kearton, 1926.

References

Abel, Richard. *Encyclopedia of Early Cinema*. London: Routledge, 2004.

Allen, D. E. *The Naturalist in Britain: A Social History*. London: Allen Lane, 1976.

Allen, Francis L. 'Early Wildlife Photographers', *Country Life*, 2 January 1937.

Baker, Steve. *Picturing the Beast: Animals Identity and Representation*. Manchester: Manchester University Press, 1993.

Beaton, Cecil. *British Photographers*. London: Collins, 1944.

Bevis, John. *Direct from Nature: The Photographic Work of Richard & Cherry Kearton*. London: Coracle, 1992; revised and enlarged edition Axminster: Colin Sackett, 2007.

Bevis, John. 'Hidden Observatories'. In *The Unpainted Landscape*, ed. Simon Cutts. London: Coracle Press, 1987.

Blackmore, M. *The Selborne Society: Its Origin and History*. London: The Selborne Society, 1985.

Bousé, Derek. *Wildlife Films*. Penn: University of Pennsylvania Press, 2000.

Bridges, Thomas & Tiltman, Hubert Hessell. *Heroes of Modern Adventure*. London: Harrap, 1932. Ch.XII 'Cherry Kearton and his Camera in Africa'.

Bright, Martin. *100 Years of Wildlife*. London: BBC Books, 2007.

Brower, Matthew. *Developing Animals: Wildlife and Early American History*. Minneapolis: University of Minnesota Press, 2011.

Buchanan, Angus. *Three Years of War in East Africa*. London: John Murray, 1919.

Cameron, Kenneth M. *Africa on Film: Beyond Black and White*. New York: Continuum, 1994.

Cameron, Kenneth M. *Into Africa: The Story of the East African Safari*. London: Constable, 1990.

Carwardine, Mark. 'Origins of Wildlife Photography'. *BBC Wildlife Magazine*, Vol.30 No.2, February 2012.

Clark, Edward B. 'Wild Life in Moving Pictures'. In *Technical World Magazine*, Vol.16, No.5, January 1912, pp.519–526.

Clark, James L. *Good Hunting*. Norman, OK: University of Oklahoma Press, 1966.

Clark, James L. *Trails of the Hunted*. London: Chatto & Windus, 1929.

Clark, James L. Diaries, 1909. Unpublished. In the collection of the American Museum of Natural History.

Doughty, R. W. *Feather Fashions and Bird Preservation: A Study in Nature Protection*. Berkeley, Los Angeles: University of California Press, 1975.

Dugmore, Arthur Radclyffe. *Camera Adventures in the African Wilds*. New York: Doubleday, Page, 1910.

Ellison, Norman F. 'A memory of Richard and Cherry Kearton'. *The Yorkshire Dalesman*, November 1945, pp.176–177.

Evans, D. E. *A History of Nature Conservation in Britain*. 2nd ed. London: Routledge, 1997.

Frost, Christopher. *A History of British Taxidermy*. Long Melford: The author, 1987.

Gardner, Joseph L. *Departing Glory: Theodore Roosevelt as ex-president*. New York: Scribner, 1973.

Gouyon, Jean-Baptiste. 'From Kearton to Attenborough: Fashioning the Telenaturalist's Identity'. *History of Science*, Vol.49 (1): pp.25–60, 2011.

Guggisberg, C. A. W. *Early Wildlife Photographers*. Newton Abbot: David & Charles, 1977.

Gunning, Tom. 'The Cinema of Attractions: Early film, its spectator and the avant-garde'. *Early Cinema: Space Frame Narrative*, ed. Thomas Elsaesser. London: British Film Institute, pp.56–62, 1990.

Hardy, Eric. 'Early Photographs of Birds'. *Country Life*, 9 May 1952, 111: pp.1417–18.

Hartley, Jean. *Africa's Big Five and Other Wildlife Filmmakers: A Centenary of Wildlife Filming in Kenya*. Nairobi: Twaweza Communications, 2010.

Hartley, Marie & Ingilby, Joan. *Yorkshire Portraits*. London: J. M. Dent, 1961.

Hasegawa, Shiori. *Sensational Africa: Roosevelt's Cultural Politics and Expeditional Filmmaking of 1909–1910*. Tsukuba: University of Tsukuba, 2010.

Hibbins, Vivien. 'With Cherry Kearton in the Loose Valley'. *Bygone Kent*, Vol.16 No.6, June 1995, pp.341–344.

Hosking, E. *An Eye for a Bird*. London: Hutchinson, 1970.

Hosking, E. & Lowes, Harold. *Masterpieces of Bird Photography*. London: Collins, 1947.

Hosking, E. & Newberry, C. *Intimate Sketches from Bird Life*. London: Country Life, 1940.

Hosking, E. & Newberry, C. *The Art of Bird Photography*. London: Country Life, 1944.

Imperato, Pascal James, & Imperato, Eleanor M. *They Married Adventure: The Wandering Lives of Martin and Osa Johnson*. New Brunswick: Rutgers University Press, 1992.

Jones, Jeannette Eileen. "In Brightest Africa': Naturalistic Constructions of Africa in the American Museum of Natural History, 1910–1936'. In *Images of Africa: Stereotypes & Realities*, ed Daniel M. Mengara. Trenton, NJ: Africa World Press, 2001, pp.195–208.

Jordan, Anne. 'The Keartons—First naturalist photographers'. *Photo Technique*, Vol.2 No.10, August 1974.

Kearton, Cherry II. 'The Keartons of Caterham'. *The Bourne Society Local History Records*, Vol.VI, 1967, pp.15–20.

Kearton, Richard, ed. Fookes, Gwyneth. *The First Bird Photographer: Richard Kearton's Field Notes for Surrey 1899–1927*. Bourne Society for private circulation, 1997.

Kearton, Richard. 'Natural History Photography'. *Pearson's Magazine*, Vol.3 No.6, June 1900: pp.466–472.

Keil, Charlie & Stamp, Shelly (ed.). *American cinema's transitional era: Audiences, institutions, practices*. Berkeley: University of California Press, 2004.

Kersey, Ralph T. *Buffalo Jones*. Garden City, KA: Elliott, 1958.

Lahue, Kalton C. 'Scientific Nature-Faking'. *Collier's*, Vol.43, 3 July 1909, p.13.

Low, Rachel. *History of the Cinema*, Vol.I: 1906–1914; Vol.II: 1914–18. London: Taylor & Francis, 1997.

Lundeberg, A., & Seymour, F. *The Great Roosevelt African Hunt and the Wild Animals of Africa*. Chicago: D. B. McCurdy, 1910.

Lutts, Ralph H. *The Nature Fakers: Wildlife, Science and Sentiment*. London: Fulcrum, 1990.

Marchington & Clay. *An Introduction to Bird and Wildlife Photography*. London: Faber, 1974.

Miller, J. M. *Hunting Big Game in the Wilds of Africa: Continued Thrilling Adventures of the Famous Roosevelt Expedition*. Washington: National Pub. Co. 1910.

Mitchell, Robert W., Thompson, Nicholas S., & Miles, H. Lyn. *Anthropomorphism, Anecdotes and Animals*. New York: SUNY Press, 1997.

Mitchell, W. R. 'Richard Kearton: Naturalist Extraordinary'. *The Dalesman*, April & May 1977.

Mitchell, W. R. 'Letters from a Dales Naturalist'. *Yorkshire Journal*, No.8, Winter 1994.

Mitchell, W. R. *Watch the Birdie!: The Life and Times of Richard and Cherry Kearton, Pioneers of Wildlife Photography*. Settle: Castleberg, 2001.

Mitchell, W. R. 'A pioneer and an inspiration'. *Yorkshire Post*, 24 February 2007.

Mitman, Gregg. *Reel Nature: America's Romance with Wildlife on Film*. Harvard University Press, 1999.

Morris, P. A. *Rowland Ward: Taxidermist to the World*. Ascot: The author, 2003.

Morris, R. F. O. *A History of British Birds*. London: John C. Nimmo, 1857.

Nowell-Smith, Simon. *The House of Cassell 1848–1958*. London: Cassell, 1958.

O'Laughlin, J. C. *From the Jungle through Europe with Roosevelt*. Boston: Chapple Pub. Co., Ltd, 1910.

Packham, Roger & Fookes, Gwyneth. 'Richard Kearton'. *Bulletin of the Bourne Society*, 1999, 178: pp.31–33.

Petterson, Palle Bøgelund. *Cameras into the Wild: A History of Early Wildlife and Expedition Filmmaking, 1895–1928*. McFarland, 2011.

Pierssene, A. S. D. 'Photographs in Victorian Bird Books', *Country Life*, 1964, 136: p.197.

Pike, O. G. *Nature Photography*. London: Chapman & Hall, 1931.

Pike, O. G. 'Early Photographs of Bird Life', *Photographic Journal*, Section A, July 1951, 91: pp.200–210.

Pitt, Frances. 'The Rise of Nature Photography', *Country Life*, 1953, 114: 1953–3.

Roosevelt Memorial Association. *Annual Report*. 1926: 18.

Roosevelt, Kermit. *A Sentimental Safari*. New York: Knopf, 1963.

Roosevelt, Theodore. *African Game Trails*. New York: Charles Scribner's Sons, 1910.

Roosevelt, Theodore. *Letters*, Vols.VI and VII.

Samstag, T. *For Love of Birds. The story of the Royal Society for the Protection of Birds 1889–1988*. Sandy, Beds: Royal Society for the Protection of Birds, 1988.

Scull, Guy H. *Lassoing Wild Animals in Africa*. New York: Stokes, 1911.

Seymour, F. *Roosevelt in Africa*. Chicago: Educational Co. 1909.

Sheail, J. *Nature in Trust: The History of Nature Conservation in Britain*. London & Glasgow: Blackie, 1976.

Snell, F. C. *The camera in the fields: a practical guide to nature photography*. London: Fisher Unwin, 1905.

Springer, Claudia. 'Watch the Birdie: Image-making and Wildlife Conservation'. *Explorations in Media Ecology*, Vol.10, 1 & 2 (2011): pp.7–23.

Stamp, S. L. D. *Nature Conservation in Britain*. New Naturalist Vol.49. London: Collins, 1969.

Thompson, J. Lee. *Theodore Roosevelt Abroad: Nature, Empire, and the Journey of an American President*. New York: Palgrave Macmillan, 2010.

Tobias, Ronald B. *Film and the American Moral Vision of Nature: Theodore Roosevelt to Walt Disney*. East Lansing: Michigan State University Press, 2011.

Turner, E. S. *All Heaven in a Rage*. London: Michael Joseph, 1964.

Tyrell, Ian. 'To the Halls of Europe: The African Safari and Roosevelt's Campaign to Conserve Nature (While Killing It)'. In *Crisis of the Wasteful Nation: Empire and Conservation in Theodore Roosevelt's America*. Chicago: Unversity of Chicago Press, 2015.

Unger, Frederick W. *Roosevelt's African Trip*. New York: W. E. Scull, 1909.

Vidal, John. 'Travels with a Shammy Leather', *Guardian*, 4 February 1994.

Wilson, Robert L. *Theodore Roosevelt, Outdoorsman*. New York: Winchester, 1971.

Winston, Thomas Pillsbury. 'A Critique of the Environmental Savior Trope in Wildlife Film'. Thesis. Bozeman, Montana: Montana State University, 2010.

Yeates, G. K. *Bird Photography*. London: Faber, 1946.

Acknowledgements

I would like to thank the following individuals for correspondence, assistance and encouragement: Mrs Margaret Bentham; the late Les Coleman; Alec Connah; Simon Cutts; Paul Goodman, National Media Museum; Marie Hartley and Joan Ingilby; Mark Haworth-Booth; Ray Howgego; Dr Cherry Kearton; Andy Mitchell; Dr W. R. Mitchell; Chester Murray; Michael Rhodes, Yorkshire Post Newspapers; Philip Sturrock, past Chairman, Cassell plc; Erica Van Horn; John Vidal; Greville Worthington.

I am grateful to the following institutions for making their resources available and responding to my enquiries: Department of Library Services, American Museum of Natural History; BBC Sound Archive; British Film Institute; British Library; British Newspaper Archive; Dales Countryside Museum; Dalesman Publishing Co. Ltd; Theodore Roosevelt Collection, Harvard College Library; Department of Documents, Imperial War Museum; Library of Congress; National Media Museum; Department of Library and Information Services, Natural History Museum; The Patent Office; Public Records Office; Royal Geographical Society; Swaledale Museum; J. B. Priestley Library, University of Bradford; Zoological Society of London; and the invaluable resources of the various public libraries in England and Northern Ireland where the bulk of this book was written. I have found Ancestry.com very useful for accessing censuses, registers, certificates of birth, marriage and death, telephone directories, shipping records, etc.

I have attempted to track down original material and to contact copyright holders. Original Kearton negatives and prints from the 1890s and early 1900s are, as Eric Hosking wrote in the introduction to *Masterpieces of Bird Photography*, surprisingly hard to locate. The writing and photographs of both brothers being now out of copyright, and the original publisher of their most significant books, Cassell, having told me they have no interest in the Keartons, I have quoted from the books and used the printed plates as source for the illustrations in this book. I'm grateful to Mrs Gwyneth Fookes, of the Bourne Society, for giving me permission to quote from the typescript which she painstakingly prepared from Richard Kearton's field notes.

I have tried to verify the facts and justify the opinions that appear in this book as far as possible. Any mistakes are mine.

I would particularly like to thank Colin Sackett for suggesting this book in the first place, and for the expertise which he and Bethan Sackett-Thomas have brought to bear in steering it through editing, formatting, design and publication; and Linda Blud, for her never ending support.

Illustrations are from *The Adventures of Cock Robin and His Mate*: p.23; *The Adventures of Jack Rabbit*: pp. 21, 76, 77; *Adventures with Animals and Men*: pp.28, 115, 127, 136, 158, 166; *The Animals Came to Drink*: p.131; *At Home with Wild Nature*: pp.60, 79; *British Birds' Nests*: pp.36, 39, 53, 146; *Keartons' Nature Pictures*: pp.9, 46, 82, 84, 100, 139, 149, 150, 172, 176; *My Dog Simba*: p.106; *My Happy Family*: p.161; *My Woodland Home*: pp.32, 33, 81, 140; *A Naturalist's Pilgrimage*: p.180; *Nature Memories* (John Kearton): p.26; *On Safari*: pp.116, 119, 120, 132, 135; *Our Bird Friends*: pp.70, 71, 74; *Our Rarer British Breeding Birds*: pp.14, 40, 54; *Pearson's Magazine*, Vol.3, No.6: p.13; *Penguin Island*: pp.162, 165; *Photographing Wild Life across the World*: pp.124, 144, 157; *Strange Adventures in Dicky Bird Land*: p.175; *Technical World Magazine*, Vol.16, No.5: p.22; *Wild Life at Home*: pp.10, 25, 45, 49, 59, 73, 87, 88, 92; *Wild Life across the World*: pp.31, 109, 110, 113, 123; *Wild Nature's Ways*: pp.62, 63, 65, 66, 91, 95, 96, 99, 103, 128, 143, 179; *With Nature and a Camera*: pp.2, 18, 43, 50, 56, 69, 153, 154; the author: p.35.

Index

Access to the countryside:
Access to Mountains Bill (1884), 48;
Commons Preservation Society, 48;
Countryside & Rights of Way Act (2000),
48; Law of Property Act (1925), 48; Local
Government Act (1894), 48; National
Footpaths Preservation Society, 48;
National Parks and Access to the
Countryside Act (1949), 49; Open Spaces
Society, 48; Wildlife and Countryside
Act (1981), 49
Achnacarry, Lochaber, Highlands, 48
Ailsa Craig, Firth of Clyde, 48
Akeley, Carl, 108, 111; *In Brightest Africa*,
119–120
Alhambra Theatre, London, 82, 125
American Museum of Natural History, 116
Animals:
adder, *150*, 151; antelope, 115; bear
(black), 28; bear (grizzly) 156; bison,
28, 156; buffalo, 116, 156; bushbuck,
155, 156; cheetah, 116, *120*, 160;
chimpanzee, 133, 160–162, *161*; cougar,
156; crocodile, *28*, 116; dog, *31*, *33*, *158*;
dolphin (spinner), 102; eland, 160;
elephant (African), 112, 115, 116, *135*;
fox, 102, 155, *175*; gazelle, 104; giraffe,
115, 116, 122, 160, *166*; gorilla, 33; grass
snake, 8–10, 151; hare, *11*; hartebeest,
160; hedgehog, 75; hippopotamus, 115,
116, 117, 122; hyena, 114, 116; jackal,
114, 155; kongoni, 104; leopard, 115,
116, 155; lion, 28, 112, 114, 115, 116, *116*,
117, 118, 122, 131–133, *131*, *132*, 134, 141,
142–145, 160; lizard, 142; mongoose,
160; monkey (grey), 160; monkey (red
colobus), *106*, 142, 156; moose, 28; musk-
ox, 156; orang-outang, 28; python, 155;
rabbit, 78, 151, 152, *179*; rhinoceros
(black), 116, 160; rhinoceros (white),
20, 114, 115, 116, 117–118, *119*, 126, *157*;
slowworm, 151; springhare, 114, 155;
squirrel, *79*; stoat, *179*; toad, 151; trout,
149; warthog, 156, 159–160; waterbuck,
115; wildebeest, 104, 115; wolf (Iberian),
141; zebra (Grévy's), 116; zebra (plains),
104, *115*, 116, 155, 160
Arras, 23
Ashby, Eric, 8, 16, 34, 142
Atlantic Monthly, 110
Attenborough, David, 8, 16, 34, 163
Audubon Society, 148

Barnes, James, 28–29, 114
Bass Rock, Firth of Forth, 48
BBC:
Bush House, 33; *Desert Island Discs*, 33;
Dolphins: Spy in the Pod, 102; *I Remember*,
33; *Nation on Film: Kearton's Wildlife*, 142
Beaton, Cecil, 55
Beecham, Sir Thomas, 31
Bentham, Howard, 23, 34, 35, 85
Bioscope, 125
Birds, nests and eggs:
arctic skua, 102; arctic tern, 48; barn
owl, 86; black tern, 38, 151; blackbird,
61, 71, *74*, 75, 94, 129, 152, 154; black-
footed penguin, 162–167, *162*, *165*;
black-throated diver, *180*; blue tit, *53*;
bullfinch, 89, 129; butcher bird, 57;
buzzard, 52; chaffinch, 61, 71, 94, 129,
154; common tern, 48, 83; common
whitethroat, 2, 129; cormorant, 48, 83,
124, 155; corncrake, 48, *55*, 75; crow,
151; cuckoo, 61, *82*, 83, 129; curlew,
98–101; Dartford warbler, *cover*; dipper,
98; dunlin, 154; eider duck, 48, *143*;
fulmar, 67, 151; gannet, 48, 75, 78, 83,
155; garden warbler, 61; golden eagle,
48; golden plover, *100*, 101; great auk,
151; great bittern, 151; great bustard,
151; great skua, 48; great tit, *140*, 152,
153; greater-spotted woodpecker,
75; greenfinch, 94, 155; grouse, *19*;
guillemot, 48, 83; gull, 25, 38; heron,
75, 155; hooded crow, 38; hoopoe, 38;
house sparrow, 94; Indian shama, 80;
jackdaw, *26*; Jackson's widowbird, 122,
130; jay, *40*, 55, 94, 95, 151; kestrel,
172; kingfisher, *50*, 52, 86, *104*, 122;
kittiwake, 48, *59*; knot, 86; lapwing, 38,
70, 93; lesser whitethroat, 129; little
owl, 151; longtailed tit, 71; magpie,
151; mallard, 86; Marabou stork, 122;
marsh harrier, 71; meadow pipit, 61, 97,
101; merlin, 93, 97–98; missel thrush,
70; Montagu's harrier, 71; mute swan,
38, *146*; nightingale, 27, 80, *81*, *128*;
nightjar, *76–77*, 129, 130; northern hawk
owl, 151; nuthatch, *15*, 55; osprey, 48;
owl, 38; oystercatcher, *46*, 101–102,
103; partridge, 75, 151, 154; passenger
pigeon, 150; peregrine, 52; pheasant,
71, 94; puffin, *39*, 48, 67, 83, 151, 155;
red grouse, 20; red-legged partridge,

86, 152; red-necked phalarope, 8; redstart, 93; ring dove, 94, 96; ringed plover, *70–71*, 75, 102; robin, *60*, 71, 78, 129, 152, 154–155; rook, 71, 129, 130; sanderling, 86; sandpiper, 93, 97; sandwich tern, 48; shag, *45*; shelduck, 48; siskin, 86; skylark, 61, 91–92, 93, 129; song thrush, 27, *36*, 37, 43, 57, 61, 64, *65*, 71, 77, 80, 94, 129, 141, 153–154; sparrowhawk, 8, *9*, 83; St Kilda wren, 67; starling, *70–71*, 75, 77, 154; stock dove, 94; swallow, 152, 154; swift, 52, 75; tree pipit, *82*, 129; turtle dove, 94, 96; vulture, 122; wheatear, 57, 93, 97, *99, 176*; white stork, 38; white-tailed eagle, 48, 151; willow warbler, 61; woodcock, 86; woodpecker, 122; wood pigeon, 71; wren, *frontis*, 67, 152; wryneck, 8, *84*, 89, 129, 130; yellowhammer, 94, *139*
Birds, accidents to, *154*, 155
Birds' nests, 51; in strange places, *60*, 152
Birdsong, 76–78, 129–130
Birkbeck Institute, 20
Board of Inventions & Research, 25
Boston, Mass, 111
Bourne Society, 15
Bousé, Derek, 163–164; *Wildlife Films*, 163
Breeding birds, distribution, 47, 55
British Ornithologists' Club, 82
Bronx Park Zoological Gardens, 160
Browning, Robert, 77
Burroughs, John, 110

Cameras and photographic equipment: *13, 25*, 35, *43, 50, 56, 69*: Aeroscope camera, 33; celluloid film, 43; Dallmeyer, 44; Demon Detective Camera, 42; dry-gel paper plate, 44; Eastman Kodak, 42–43; miniature camera used as view-finder, 44; Thornton & Pickard, 44; wet collodion plate, 44
Camouflage, 12
Cassell & Co, Ltd. (ex Cassell, Petter & Galpin): 20–21, 22, 26, 34, 41–42; editor Lewis Wright, 41; eminent authors, 21; La Belle Sauvage, 20, 34, 44
Chapman, Frank Michler, 103
Cherry Kearton Films Ltd, 33
Cherry Kearton Ltd, 32–33, 121; *The Whirlpool of War*, 33
Cherry Kearton Medal & Award (Royal Geographical Society), 34
Cherry, Agnes, 20
Cheyne Court, Romney Marsh, 49
Chicago, 112
Chislett, Ralph, 8
Clark, James L., 28, 114, 117–118, 142, 155–156
Coates, Calvert, 27
Coates, William James, 28, 34, 107, 112, 117, 118, 155–156

Coates, William, 27
Cole, Berkeley, 132–133, 145
Collecting, 114, 115–117, 149–150, 155–156
Collier's magazine, 117
Conrad, Joseph, *Heart of Darkness*, 119
Conservation, 15, 16, 48–49, 108, 117, 141, 148–151, 156
Cook, Captain James, 58–59
Cumbria, 19:
    Brough, 21; Eden Valley, 93; Kirkby Stephen, 20, 97; Mallerstang, 23; Nateby, 22, 61; Nateby Fell, 97–98; Potts Valley, 93, 98, 101

Daily Chronicle, 137
Daisies Asleep, Daisies Awake, *62–63*, 63–64
Dales Countryside Museum, Hawes, 35
Dassen Island, 162–167
Dawson, Warrington, 111
de Vries, Herman, 12, 71
Dew pond, 94–95
Direct from Nature, 16
Drury, Chris, 12
Dugmore, Arthur Radclyffe, 117

East Africa, 108, 109:
    Kijabe, 142; Kiu, 121; Lake Naivasha, 117, 122; Luna Park, 121–122; Mombasa, 29, 107, 111, 121, 138; Mount Kenya, 118; Nairobi, 109, 112, 117; Norfolk Hotel, 112, 118; Railway Institute, 118; Nakuru, 121; Nyeri, 118, 120, 142; Sultan Hamud, 117
East Finchley Congregational Literary Society, 25
Edendale, Los Angeles, 112
Edison:
    Edison Bell wax cylinder recorder, 80; Edison Manufacturing Company, 111
Edmondsley, Co. Durham, 22
Elizabeth, New Jersey, 125
Elsbury, Martin, 142, 144
Enculturation, 161–162
Enfield, Middlesex, *36*, 37, 38, 43

Farne Islands, *38*, 48
Farren, William, 82
Fortune, Riley, 68
Fothergill, Alastair, 163
Frontiersmen, Legion of, 29; eminent members, 29–30
Fulton, Hamish, 12

Galpin, Sydney, 20
German East Africa, 29
Gobbett, D. W. 'Dave', 156, 159
Gouyon, Jean-Baptiste, 114
Greenwell, Walpole, 91

Heller, Edmund, 111
Herrick, Francis, 103
Hewins, Charles A., 38

Hides, 7, 24, 85–105:
artificial block of ice, 102; artificial
elephant dung, 102; artificial rock, 98–
101; artificial rubbish heap, 92–93, 92;
artificial tree-trunk, 87–88, 89; dummy
zebra, 104–105; heather house, 97–98;
reed-covered punt, 102; reversible suit,
86–89; spy dolphin, 102; spy ray,102;
spy sea turtle, 102; spy tuna, 102; stone
house, 101–102, 103; stuffed ox, 8–9,
12, 17, 90–96, 91, 95; stuffed sheep,
96–97, 96, 105; tent hide, 103; turf hovel
(sod house), 102; umbrella blind, 103;
wooden door, 86; wooden mask, 89
Hoffman, H. F., 125
Hollywood, 112, 125
Hosking, Eric, 8, 11, 34; Masterpieces of Bird
Photography, 11
Hunt, William Henry 'Birds Nest', 52
Hutchinson & Co., 24

Insects, 72–74:
beetle, 72; bluebottle, 72; moth, 72–75;
red admiral, 72; small tortoiseshell
butterfly, 73

Jackson, Sir Frederick, 118, 120
Jarrold Publishing, 24
Johnson, Martin & Osa, 127
Johnston, Burgoyne, 34
Jones, Charles 'Buffalo', 28, 114, 144–145,
156–160, 157

Kearton, Ada Louisa, née Forrest (CK's
wife), 30, 31–32, 33, 34, 35, 37, 62, 127,
129, 133–134, 137–138, 155, 160–163,
167; m. Allen Hawes, 31; On Safari, 33,
62, 129, 133, 134, 137; Penguin Island,
33, 133; The Cherry Kearton Animal Book,
33, 133; Under African Skies, 33, 133
Kearton, Cherry (grandfather), 20
Kearton, Cherry (RK's grandson), 35
Kearton, Cherry 'Plod', 'Cherry Kearton II'
(RK's son), 21, 22, 24, 25, 34, 151; m.
Doris Baines, 24
Kearton, Cherry, 13, 28, 33, 45, 49, 50, 56, 69,
87, 95, 106, 113, 136, 162:
upbringing, 16, 19–20, 21; character,
57–59; employment, 22, 26–27;
marriage and family, 27, 30–32, 33–34,
61; war service, 29–30. Writing, 9,
121, 130, 133–136, 138–139, 163;
photography, 8, 9, 24, 26–27, 37–38,
42–44, 49, 51–55, 68–69, 152, 167;
lecturing, 9, 27; film, 8, 16, 27, 28–29,
80–83, 126–127, 142–145, 159–160,
163–164; sound recording, 8, 27, 32,
80. Visits: Algeria, 27, 32; Australia, 32,
137; Belgium, 29; Borneo, 28; Canada,
28; East Africa, 27–28, 29–30, 32, 107,
112–121; Egypt, 32; India, 28; Indonesia,

32; Morocco, 32; New Zealand, 32;
Sahara, 32; Scandinavia, 27; Singapore,
28; South Africa, 31, 32, 162–164;
USA, 28. Publications: Adventures with
Animals and Men, 30, 135–136, 163–164;
Cherry Kearton's Travels, 138; In the Land
of the Lion, 138; The Island of Penguins,
133, 163; I Visit the Antipodes, 58–59;
My Animal Friendships, 133, 161; My
Dog Simba, 133; My Friend Toto, 133;
My Happy Chimpanzee, 133; My Happy
Family, 161; My Woodland Home, 138,
141; Photographing Wild Life across the
World, 121, 130–133, 134, 144; Shifting
Sands of Algeria, 133, 138; Wild Life
Across the World, 130–133, 137, 138,
141–142, 145, 156. Films: Dassen, 8; Our
grip on the Huns in East Africa, 30; A
Primitive Man's Career to Civilization,
126; Roosevelt in Africa, 28, 121–126; Sea
Bird Colonies, 83; Tembi, 127; Wild Birds
at Home, 83.
Kearton, Dora (RK's daughter), 23, 34, 91
Kearton, Edward Cherry (CK's son), 27,
31; m. Patience Geraldine I. Wood, 27;
daughter Morella, 27
Kearton, Ellen Rose, née Cowdrey (RK's
wife), 23, 26, 89, 153
Kearton, Foster (brother), 19, 21–22; m.
Jane Brunskill, 21, family, 21; Emma
Atkinson and family, 21–22
Kearton, Grace (RK's daughter), 23, 23,
24, 34, 66, 91, m. Howard Bentham, 23;
daughter Margaret, 23
Kearton, Jane (sister) 19, 21, 22; daughter
Ann, 22–23
Kearton, John (brother) 19, 21, 22; m.
Frances Adelaide Bullock, 23–34, 86;
son Cherry, 23; niece Marjorie Crerar, 34
Kearton, John 'Jack' (father), 19, 21
Kearton, John 'Jack' (RK's son), 21, 22,
24, 34, 57; Bird Life in England, 24;
Nature Memories, 24, 57; Nature Smiling
Through, 24
Kearton, Margaret (sister), 19, 22, 23
Kearton, Mary Burwood, née Coates (CK's
wife), 27, 30, 31, 61, 130, 145; m. George
M. Style, 30
Kearton, Mary Nina 'Nina' (CK's daughter),
27, 31; m. Montague Simpson, 27
Kearton, Mary, née Hunter (mother), 19,
21, 22–23
Kearton, Richard 'Dick' (RK's son), 21, 22,
23–24, 34; m. Minnie Elizabeth Cobb, 24
Kearton, Richard, 22, 26, 56, 69:
upbringing, 16, 19–20; character, 59–61;
employment, 20–21, 24; marriage and
family, 23–24, 26, 33–34. Writing, 8, 9,
24, 41–42, 50–51, 155; photography, 9,
24, 63–66, 68–69, 95–96, 152, 167; film,
82–83; lecturing, 9, 24–25, 26; fieldwork,

25, 61, 69–72, 129, 152–155. Visits:
Berlin, 25; Netherlands, 25; Norway,
25; Paris, 25; USA, 25. Publications: *The
Adventures of Cock Robin and His Mate*, 78;
The Adventures of Jack Rabbit, 78; *At Home
with Wild Nature*, 153, 155; *Baby Birds at
Home*, 80, 153; *Birds' Nests, Eggs, and Egg
Collecting*, 24, 41; *British Birds' Nests*, 8,
16, 24, 37–55, 86, 149; *The Fairyland of
Living Things*, 79–80, 130; *A Naturalist's
Pilgrimage*, 26, 37; *Our Bird Friends*, 79;
Our Rarer British Breeding Birds, 55, 78–
79; *The Pocket Book of British Birds*, 85–86;
Richard Kearton's Field Diaries, 61, 69–72,
129–130; *Strange Adventures in Dicky Bird
Land*, 78; *Wild Bird Adventures*, 78; *Wild
Life at Home*, 63, 86, 153; *Wild Nature's
Ways*, 7, 7, 63, 85, 93, 147; *With Nature
and a Camera*, 25, 62–63, 67, 86, 151–152;
Wonders of Wild Nature, 147.
Kennedy, Alexander Charles, 38
Kikuyu, 120, 122, 123
Kington, Herefordshire, 27
Klein, Yves, 12
Koch, Ludwig, 80

Lassoing animals, 28, 130–131, 142, 145,
152, 156–160, 157
Liberia, 24
Little Folks Magazine, 42
Live Stock Journal, 42
Liverpool, 111
Lodge, Reginald B., 11, 38, 44, 82
London Daily News, 137
London Zoo, 151, 161
London, Jack, 110
London:
Boreham Wood, 8, 23, 27; Bush House,
33; Cecil Court, 159; Charing Cross
Road, 33; Clapham High Street, 33; East
Finchley, 25; Edmonton, 23; Factory
Lane, Croydon, 137; Fleet Street, 42;
Hammersmith, 23; Hampstead Way, 33;
Hommerton, 90; Hornsey Park Road, 22,
23; Kentish Town, 90; Malvern Road, 22;
Marylebone, 31; Mill Hill, 34; Norwood,
137; Paddington, 33; Pagani's Restaurant,
Great Portland Street, 82; Piccadilly, 89–
90, 109; Smithfield, 23; South Norwood,
27; St Johns Wood, 31, 160; St Paul's
Cathedral, 134, 136; Streatham, 137; Tite
Street, Chelsea, 30; Wandsworth Gas
Works, 134, 136; Wardour Street, 134;
Wood Street, 27, 34
Long, Richard, 12
Long, William J., 110
Loring, J. Alden, 111, 115
Loveless, Marshall, 156
Lowe, Frank, 60
Lowes, Harold, 11
Lydon, Alexander Francis, 41

Madrid, 141
Manhattan, 107
Mansell-Pleydell, J. C., 38
Masai, 28, 120, 122, 132, 132–134, 143–148,
144, 159
Means, Ambrose, 156
Mearns, Edgar A., 111
Mitchell, W. R., 15, 35; The W. R. Mitchell
Archive, 35; *Watch the Birdie!*, 15, 35
Mitman, Greg, 164
Morris, Revd Francis Orpen, 41, 51
Motion Picture Patents Company, 125
Moving Picture World, 121, 122, 125
Mull, Inner Hebrides, 48
Murray, Chester, 35
Muybridge, Edweard, 38, 75

Naples, 107, 111
National Media Museum, Bradford, 35
National Trust, 48–49; Wicken Fen, 49
Natural History Museum, London, 12–13,
35, 50, 141, 149
Nature photography books, early, 38
New York Natural History Museum, 28, 117
Nickelodeon, 121
North Uist, Outer Hebrides, 48, 54, 101

Over, Jeremy, 12

Pathé Frères, 121, 122
Photographic pairs and sequences, 62–63,
63–64, 67, 74, 75–76, 76–77, 83
Pike, Oliver G., 38, 83, 147
Plants, 71:
daisy, 63–64, 62–63, 72, 83, 152;
dandelion, 72, 83, 152; great mullein,
75–76; primrose, 66–67, 66
Populism, 12–13
Potter, Beatrix, 78
Pownall, Colonel H. R., 29
*Primroses photographed in the first moments
of the twentieth century*, 66–67, 66
Printing:
gravure, 44–47; half-tone, 47
Putsborough, Devon, 30
Reynoldson, John George, 34
Rodriguez, Jose Luis, 141
Roosevelt, Kermit, 109, 111, 115, 116
Roosevelt, Theodore, 25, 28, 107–127, 113:
African Game Trails, 109; Boone &
Crockett Club, 108; 'Education in Africa',
118–119; *Good Hunting*, 110; *ingoma* at
Nyeri, 120–121; National Progressive
Party, 126; naturalist, 107–108; nature
faking, 109–111; 1912 election, 126; on
safari, 115–117; President of USA, 107
Royal Flying Corps, 24, 30
Royal Naval Air Service, 30
RSPB (formerly Society for the Protection
of Birds), 49, 148

Safari, 27–28, 32, 58, 107, 108–127, *109*, *110*
Saltee Islands, Ireland, 48
Science Museum, London, 35
Scott, Peter, 8
Scottish Arts Council, 12
Scull, Guy H., 159
Selig, William, 111, 112, 141:
    Roosevelt in Africa, 112; *Hunting Big
    Game in Africa*, 112
Selous, Frederick C., 29, 58, 108, 111
Seton, Ernest Thompson, 110
Sharpe, Richard Bowdler, 50, 51, 68
Shepard, E. H., 78
Shetland:
    Unst, *44*, 48, *49*; Noup of Noss, *59*
Ships:
    Bardistan, 107; *Hamburg*, 107; *Ivernia*,
    111; *Llanstephan Castle*, 31; *Titanic*, 57
Slade, Irene, 33
Smith, F. Percy, 83
Smith, Stuart, 8
Smithsonian Institution, 107, 109, 126
Sound recording, 8, 27, 32, 80, *81*
Southampton, 107
Southport, 38
Speaker, 42
Spencer Brothers, 27, 134–137, *136*:
    Henry, 134; Herbert, 134, 136–137;
    Percival, 134; Stanley, 134
St Kilda, 67, 78, 83, 151
Stanley, H. M., 119; *In Darkest Africa*, 119
Substance, Shadow and Reflection, 64–66, *65*
Surrey:
    Caterham, 24, 66, 151: 'Ardingley Villas',
    24, 91–92, 'Ashdene', 24, 34, St Mary's
    Church, 33–34, 'Kearton Court', 34,
    Marden Park, 91; Coulsdon, 33; Godstone,
    27, 61; Kenley, 7, 27, 80, *81*, 129: 'The
    Jungle', 32, *32*, 34, 'Kearton Close',
    34; Kingston Hill, 27; Kingswood, 34;
    Merstham, 27; Purley, 24; Tadworth, 23
Swaledale, 19:
    Buttertubs Pass, 20; Gunnerside, 23,
    27; Muker, 19, 21, 22–23, 34: National
    School, 19, 34; Shunnerfell, 101;
    Thwaite, 19, 27, 34, *35*
Swaysland, Walter, 41, 51
Sydney Morning Herald, 137

Taxidermy and taxidermists, 28, 89–91, 97,
    107, 108, 109, 117, 149, 152
Theodore Roosevelt's Arrival in Africa, 112
Thoreau, Henry David, 147
Thorpe, Charles, 97, 98
Thurston, Gavin, 142
Tobias, Ronald B., 126
Torquay, Devon, *14*
Tovil, Kent, 32, 34, 161

Ulyate, Ray, 156, 159
University of Bradford, J. B. Priestley
    Library, 35
Unpainted Landscape, 12
Urban, Charles, 27, 32, 134
Usher, John, 49

Wakamba, 127, *127*
Wallihan, A. G. & Wallihan, Mary A., 103
Walwyn, Hugh, 24
Ward, Rowland, 89–90, 152
Warwick Trading Company, 32; *Warwick
    Bioscope Chronicle*, 32
White House, Washington, 25, 111
Wicken Fen, Cambridgeshire, 49
Wilberforce, William, 91
Wild Bird Protection laws, 150
Wilde, Oscar, 21
Wildlife Photographer of the Year (NHM),
    141
Wood, Sir Henry, 31
Wooden eggs, 153–154
World War I, 8, 23, 29–30
Wyles, Benjamin, 38

Yellowstone National Park, 156
Yorkshire Post, 37, 41

Zoological Photographic Club, 38
Zulu, 122